AIMING HIGHER

A JOURNEY THROUGH
MILITARY AVIATION LEADERSHIP

CHRIS STRICKLIN, ROBERT TESCHNER, JASON HARRIS,

KIM CAMPBELL, DANIEL WALKER

Library of Congress Cataloging-in-Publication Data:

Names: Stricklin, Christopher, author.

               Teschner, Robert, author.

               Harris, Jason, author.

               Campbell, Kim, author.

               Walker, Daniel, author.

Title: Aiming Higher: A Journey Through Military Aviation Leadership

Description: First edition. | Chesterfield: RTI Press, 2022.

Identifiers: ISBN: 979-8-9860371-0-3

Subjects: LCSH: Leadership. | Teamwork. | Accountability. | Teams. | Organizational effectiveness.

Printed in the United States of America

10 9 8 7 6 5 4 3 2 1

PREFACE

Military Mentorship Mastermind

Military Mentorship Mastermind is a concept founded in 2020 to continue the high-performing leadership growth and mentorship found in our United States Military for proven senior military leaders transitioning to the civilian world after a career of service to this nation. Our military is known for its ability to cultivate leaders who make life and death decisions that shape the future of this nation with limited information on accelerated timelines. Mentorship is the key secret to consistent and accelerated military leadership development.

The US military demands definitive leadership on two-year rotations with exponentially increasing levels of authority, responsibility, and accountability. Individuals are required who are both intrinsically and organizationally motivated, deliberately and routinely educated, and prepared and willing for the challenge of next-level leadership when both the lives and future of our nation is at stake. How do these individuals ensure they are prepared for the daily challenge and burden of leadership during the execution of each command assignment? The secret is to live and grow within a safety net of vertical and horizontal mentorship. Thereby, each leader stands on the shoulders of giants, encompassed by mentors who have endured the challenge before, embraced by peers who are enduring similar challenges alongside them, and empowering the next generation to follow in their footsteps.

This mindset of mentorship, when properly translated to corporate America, drives efficient and effective organizations to realize accelerated success and profits. In recent years, military professionals sought small pockets of peers in which to continue this growth. The first cohort decided to put pen to paper and share their thoughts about mentorship as a seed to grow others who are both developing their exit strategy from a military career and transitioning their military experience to the business sector. Each author in this mastermind has donated their time and works to this project. All profits will be donated to charity. It is our hope that this book sparks growth in every person who reads it and encourages them not only to achieve higher levels of success, but to devote time to developing others.

Some wake up to an alarm.

Others wake to a calling.

Find yours!

CONTENTS

CHAPTER 1

PURPOSEFUL PEERS

Perspective & Insight of
Chris Stricklin

Values lie at the heart of our story.

As each of us individually emerged into adulthood to write the story of our lives, our journeys came together collectively and definitively as we began our college chapters. On an early June morning, an Air Force blue bus arrived 7,258 feet above sea level, and the door opened with people eagerly awaiting our arrival. Shortly after walking down the three simple steps to the ground, each of us remember gazing upon the Core Values Ramp at the United

States Air Force Academy. At the time, we did not understand the impact this moment would have on each of our lives. A seemingly short walk up the meticulously constructed ramp to enter the infamous terrazzo launched an alignment of values, purpose, passion, determination, and teamwork that shaped our lives more than any other single event.

Integrity First

Service Before Self

Excellence in All We Do

We grew as military officers, fighter pilots, transport pilots, and special operations pilots. But more importantly, regardless of the differences of our trades, the similarities of our growth connected us across the years. We matured our thought processes and decision-making skills. We formed our style within the construct of life and death decisions for ourselves and others. We became the senior military leaders our nation needed us to be. Decades later, we collectively realized the foundation for our leadership skills went back to the core values instilled from day one. 'Integrity First' led us to be honest, open, and transparent leaders. 'Service Before Self' established our servant leadership styles through which we always remember our purpose is to serve others. Finally, 'Excellence in All We Do' challenged us to always be better tomorrow than we are today.

We each reached the pinnacle of our Air Force careers individually and found ourselves in unique situations. At the

Purposeful peers provide a unique growth platform, no repercussions from an open discussion, and both an expectation and requirement for truth.

end of any military career, every person is challenged to step into Life 2.0 post-military service.

To grow, evolve, and mature at the accelerated rate required for military leaders, we surround ourselves with others like ourselves...similar in purpose, passion, drive, and determination. These connections are never one-way. Rather, they require open communication with reciprocal mentorship and advice. These purposeful peers provide a unique growth platform, no repercussions from an open discussion, and both an expectation and requirement for truth. We speak truth to one another about what we did right, what we did wrong, and what we can contribute to each other behind the scenes. These relationships are only successful when professional discretion is exerted to maintain confidentiality at the proper level. More importantly, each participant must treat the relationship like a bank account, always ensuring contributions greater than the amount withdrawn. As one steps from their military world to the civilian one, the need for this mentorship and growth group becomes even more critical for success in life.

These military mentorship masterminds continue to grow in their value as each of us now find ourselves in the corporate world facing new challenges. From our complex monthly interactions grew this effort: To put pen to paper with some of our insights. We in no way purport that we have all the answers, only that we are willing to devote time to becoming greater tomorrow than we are today. And we are willing to invest in others because we know that is how we truly grow ourselves. We did not have the time to compose a manuscript, but collectively felt we would be remiss if we did not put in the effort to empower those who follow in our footsteps.

Our hope is that these simple pages will serve as seed to grow your tree of success stronger than it is today and inspire others to do the same. Our dedication is to continuous improvement. Our quest is for something we can never achieve... perfection. While we know the achievement of perfection is likely impossible, the pursuit of it ensures we come closer to achieving it each day. Perfection describes the desired result, while excellence defines the process by which we perform.

Military Mentorship Mastermind Cohort One was built deliberately. From individual monthly mentorship video calls, we formed a collective. In the spirit of Jim Rohn's logic that you are the average of the five people you spend the most time with, we sat in front of a whiteboard and began to examine people for the collective. They needed to be aligned in mission, motivation, and passion. Their credibility as senior military leaders must be unwavering, and they must be open to the concept of joining forces for the collective good with no monetary gain. From this innovative session, the group became clear. As the invitations went out, they came back even faster, each accepted with the same passion with which they were sent! The group was set, the project established, and the challenge accepted.

As you ponder the following pages, remember values lie at the heart of our story and culminate in a family—not one connected in name, but in mission, belief, passion, purpose, and dedication. It is our quest to be better tomorrow than we are today and to help others achieve self-actualization while we are on the journey to reach our true potential.

Together we can achieve more than we ever dreamed individually.

Do you accept the challenge to reach for your true potential?

CHAPTER 2

FULFILLMENT
IN LIFE

Perspective & Insight of
Chris Stricklin

Imagine you're emerging from the sanctity of a full night's rest. Your eyes crack open, welcoming the first light of tomorrow's sunrise as you realize it has become your today. Before you is a blank canvas, untouched and ready to develop into a new day's worth of memories and experiences through the brush strokes of your actions, inactions, and reactions; your decisions and indecisions; your experiences yet to come.

Stop.

Take 30 seconds and state your definition of success—out loud.

Don't think, just let instinct fill the void with how you intend to measure success. Then assess: Are you happy with your answer? Was it more difficult to put to words than you first thought, and do you need to think more deeply on this?

Now consider this: Have you ever taken the time to determine your personal definition of success for a given day? For every day? For a second of time? Ironically, few of us take time to personally define the single thing around which we design our lives. Now, many of us consider ourselves more focused on happiness than success. When defined correctly, happiness and success are one and the same.

People regularly talk about professional visions but often fail to plan their personal lives with the same effort. To truly achieve fulfillment, we must be as deliberate in our personal lives as we are in our work. Few of us have devoted the requisite time to define the single thing around which we live our lives—which means we have a HUGE opportunity before us. Seize it.

START BY DEFINING SUCCESS

Right now—as you sit here reading the words on this page—ask yourself what your picture of success looks like. Consider it both for this specific day as well as for the journey of your life. Success is something we devote our lives to achieve, yet so few are able to put into words what success truly looks like. How can you work for something your entire life and not have a clear definition of what it is? Critically, how will you know when you achieve it, or in a moment of brutally honest reflection, realize you've missed the mark?

*Fulfillment is not an
entitlement, it's an
achievement.*

The only true definition of success that matters in life is the one we choose for ourselves.

Set aside some time for a strategy session for your life and write your definition of success in one short sentence. The goal is to define it in three to five words. Make it simple, clear, definitive, and measurable. Periodically, reexamine and refine it. Above all, embrace it. It should encompass every aspect of life. This is your definition of success in life, and it is the single focus by which you should allocate your time and effort.

Success is not a destination; it is a journey. Career is what you do, not who you are. Fulfillment is not an entitlement, it's an achievement. Achievements are steppingstones, not destinations. Purpose guides fulfillment, and your 'why' determines your purpose. This leads to arguably the most important question in life, "What is my WHY?"

DETERMINE YOUR 'WHY'

To develop your 'why' in life, examine two different instances. First, fast forward to the end of the longest and hardest day of work you have ever experienced. As you are driving, possibly dirty, sweaty, and exhausted, what brings a smile to your face? What gives you the satisfaction of accomplishment and makes you say, "I can't wait to do this again tomorrow"?

Next, picture yourself on your death bed. As you inhale the final breath of your time here on earth, what is your answer to the question, "Why did I live this life?" What answer would bring eternal satisfaction to your mind as you exhale the breath of life for the final time?

The combined answer to these two questions will help you truly understand your 'why'. Your 'why' in life must be all-encompassing. It will guide professional effort, personal development, who you spend time with—as well as who you avoid—where you volunteer your effort, and the group with which you align. With each effort, action, and moment, you must continually ask, "How does this align with my 'why'? Continued alignment will help ensure you are intentional with every moment.

Now imagine this hypothetical exercise: tomorrow when you wake, I will hand you $86,400 in cash. It's yours to use as you see fit. The only rule is that you have twenty-four hours to spend the money and any remaining cash must be returned at midnight. How intentional would you be with each dollar? How would you ensure you achieved the greatest gain for every dollar spent? Imagine that, but live this: each day has 86,400 seconds, and there are no carryovers or redos. The only things you carry into each tomorrow are the memories and experiences you live on each day's journey. Why would we be more intentional with money than we are with our most precious resource? Why don't we give time the same devotion as we do our cash?

DEVELOP YOUR 'WHAT'

Now that you know the single question around which your entire life is focused, develop your plan. Define what you need to do, accomplish, or achieve to enable your 'why'.

Stand in front of a whiteboard. Draw two points with your marker. On the left side, the point defines the start of today—the beginning of your new journey. On the right side, the point defines the finish line of your life. In the space between, list the individual accomplishments and achievements of which your path will be composed. Have a hard talk with yourself about what really matters and why each item is a must-have. Under each, list the reason why it is a necessary component of your life and what the ramifications would be if you don't realize them.

BUILD YOUR 'HOW'

Gazing at the whiteboard of your life is like looking at a puzzle that hasn't yet to be fully assembled. The pieces depict today, the future, and all the experiences between. The art and intentionality are found in how you learn from yesterday and connect today to each of the tomorrows that define your future.

Start with the end in mind. Build from the right side, the finish line of life, back to today. Sequence each item in the order needed to build the journey back to where you are now and understand the deliberate, specific steps needed to accomplish each one. Ask any Olympian, combat-proven senior military officer, or best-selling author how it felt when they became successful, and each will tell you they are still on the journey to achieve their true potential. Today is the combined total of our yesterdays. It's also the starting point of our preparation for a better tomorrow.

DEBRIEF YOUR DAYS

Be honest with yourself. Set a time to debrief your journey at regular points along the way. Whether Thunderbird pilots after a show, a SEAL team after a mission, or a football team after a game, high achievers reflect on their actions and review lessons learned to improve future execution. In this same manner, each of us must examine the details of our days. No one is perfect, but the pursuit of perfection involves learning from every action, inaction, and reaction to improve our method and manner.

As you climb in bed tonight, look back on your day and ask yourself one simple question: "If this were my last day on this earth, would I have done the things I did today?" If the answer is in any way 'no', then choose a new path for tomorrow. Don't find yourself always reacting to whatever may occur in life. Instead, be proactive in the orchestration of your life and understand the way you want to live. Focus on the details of today as a step on your path to success, using the same precision a Thunderbird pilot uses to maneuver their aircraft to perfection in front of 1.2 million spectators.

THE FINISH LINE

Remember, success is a journey not a destination. The only true finish line in life is when you take your last breath. None of your worldly possessions will remain with you. The only thing you take is your heart, and it will hopefully contain the fulfillment of your purpose in this life. It will carry the answer to your 'why' into eternity. The most vital aspect of personal success is the legacy you leave behind, and that legacy is simply the manner in which you answered your 'why'.

Do not live the 86,400 seconds of each day passively. Instead, aggressively, deliberately, and intentionally live each second to its fullest. We are often asked what we would die for. The more important question is what will you live for?

Today is the result of experiences, decisions, actions, reactions, and inactions of yesterday. Both the good times and the trying ones make us who we are. Tomorrow will be the product of today's thoughts, goals, focus, and desires. Don't watch life go by and think of what could have been. Seize the day and the initiative. Be proactive and realize what life can become. Choose to embrace each and every day. Choose to invest fully in life. Live each day like it may be your last, because one day it will!

Choose to #LiveIntentionally

POINTS TO PONDER

2.1   What factors into your definition of success?

2.2   What do you live for? What is your 'why'?

2.3   List the five most important things in your life, then determine if the moments of each day are allocated correctly to those five or to other things that detract from your ability to live intentionally.

CHAPTER 3

EMBRACE FAILURE

Perspective & Insight of
Robert Teschner

A s an Air Force fighter pilot, one of the most powerful lessons each must learn as they join the ranks of the top pilots in the world is to embrace failure. That lesson drives the purpose for the work fighter pilots do each and every day.

To embrace failure means to live in discomfort.

To embrace failure is to learn to be both humble and highly vulnerable.

To embrace failure—to live through it and to consistently learn from it—is the most efficient and effective recipe for lasting success.

To embrace failure—to live through it and to consistently learn from it—is the most efficient and effective recipe for lasting success.

In order to embrace failure, we must leave ego by the wayside, and we absolutely have to learn to get over ourselves, to get out of our own way. In practice, embracing failure can be exceedingly difficult.

Of the myriad topics business leaders are mentored on, embracing failure is one of the toughest and, simultaneously, most rewarding that must be covered. The concept breaks down like this.

FAILURE ISN'T ALL BAD. IN FACT, IT'S MOSTLY GOOD.

A little insight into me: I happen to be a huge fan of the work of Dr. Amy Edmondson, Novartis Professor of Leadership and Management at the Harvard Business School. She's devoted her professional life to understanding what makes teams work and to helping organizations learn to build teams that win. She's also an advocate for the value and importance of failure in building real teams.

In her HBR article titled "Strategies for Learning from Failure," Dr. Edmondson introduces the world to what she calls 'A Spectrum of Reasons for Failure.' On one end of the spectrum, she lists events we traditionally view as blameworthy events which include both deviance and inattention. On the other end of the Spectrum, she identifies as "praiseworthy" events like hypothesis testing and exploratory testing.

And it makes sense. Let's say a person crashes the company truck because they were texting while driving. This would be a blameworthy event—an absolutely unnecessary and completely avoidable failure. On the other side of the Spectrum, let's say we're trying to figure out how to sell via Zoom in the early stages of the pandemic. Maybe we've never sold over Zoom before, and maybe our first several attempts go poorly. The fact we keep coming back, that we keep trying despite our repeated failures, is praiseworthy. In fact, it is our praiseworthy efforts to keep trying that will ultimately lead to positive change and the necessary transformation to win.

On Dr. Edmondson's Spectrum most of the reasons she lists for failure aren't of the blameworthy variety. In fact, most gravitate quickly toward praiseworthy. Specifically, she notes, "The wisdom of learning from failure is incontrovertible. Yet organizations that do it well are extraordinarily rare. This gap is not due to a lack of commitment to learning… The reason: Those managers were thinking about failure the wrong way." They do so because it's all they know: Fail and you'll be punished.

Our culture in American fighter squadrons is different.

In the flying business we learned early on that there was NO WAY we could get everything right the first, second, tenth, or perhaps even twenty-fifth time. We also learned the only way we could get to the level of performance, both expected and required, was through incremental progress, progress driven by the constant analysis of our decisions and resultant actions.

Fighter pilots are *expected* to fail, and fail we did. Repeatedly. Then we were taught to analyze and study our failures. Finally, we had to take action on what we thought we learned from our failures to improve future execution. We'd go back out, execute, and repeat. Over, and over, and over again.

Our instructors taught us to embrace the praiseworthy components of failure by modeling it through their behaviors. Our culture gave us the space to learn. The fighter squadron stressed the importance of constant learning and being intentional about analyzing our failures to maximize opportunities to grow. The fighter squadron gives us an impeccable model to replicate in business.

HOW WE DISCUSS FAILURE MATTERS TO OUR TEAM

Fighter pilots are incredibly self-critical. We beat ourselves up when we make mistakes. We instinctively feel disappointed any time our performance is less than perfect. It's part of what drives us.

When I was privileged to progress in my flying career to the point of leading others on complicated missions, I was hard on my teammates when we failed to achieve our objectives. I naturally over-emphasized mistakes and was very quick to make us all hang our heads in shame during our post-mission debriefs—the space where we analyzed our performance to learn. Early on in my evolution as a flight lead, I learned from one of my instructors that I was framing the conversation the wrong way.

After a particularly disastrous mission—one where we absolutely did not achieve mission success—I spent about three hours talking about how poorly we executed and how terribly we performed. I framed the discussion around the negative aspects. I made us all feel bad, even to the point of questioning whether we had it in us to do better in the future. This wasn't intentional; it was natural.

Once I finished berating us all for our collective deficiencies, my instructor pilot took over from me and summarized our performance as follows: "Do you realize we were two decisions away from victory today?"

He then spent a couple of minutes making sure I understood which decisions should have been made differently to enable our success. He finished by asking me if I felt confident I could make those decisions the next day. I assured him I did. He said, "Great. Now go win tomorrow!" And with that, his debrief was done.

By framing the conversation around the positive aspects of the mission— "Do you realize we were two decisions away from victory today?"—he made a positive and inspiring impact in a fraction of the time it took me to tear my team down. He also left me energized and confident that we'd have a much better outcome the next time around. And he was right. I'm proud to report that the next mission was indeed a success!

BEING ABLE TO EMBRACE FAILURE IS DEPEN-
DENT UPON HOW VULNERABLE WE'RE ALLOWED
TO BE.

It turns out the Air Force fighter squadron, specifically
the way we learn from missions that don't go well, is grounded
in a concept called Psychological Safety. Dr. Timothy Clark,
author of the book *The 4 Stages of Psychological Safety*, defines
psychological safety as "an environment of rewarded vulnerability." Vulnerability is further defined as "being able to admit
to mistakes and weaknesses in a public setting".

In fighter squadrons we learn from our earliest days as
new pilots that we need to readily admit to our failures in order
to learn quickly and improve in a dangerous and demanding
work environment. It's part of the values and belief system of
our tribe, and it's part of manifesting integrity in all we do. In
the fighter squadron our reward for being consistently vulnerable is acceptance, guidance, and focused instruction. It's also
the promise that we won't be penalized for trying our best and
not getting it right the first, second, tenth, or twenty fifth time
we attempt a new maneuver, tactic, or procedure.

The funny thing is I had never heard the term 'psychological safety' during my time in the Air Force. I came across it
when I was reverse engineering why it is that fighter squadron
teams are so consistently effective in such a demanding environment. A friend of mine—a consultant who was a couple
of years ahead of me in his transition to the corporate training
world—turned me on to the term and I began my study of it.

Dr. Clark noted that American fighter squadrons are among the most advanced practitioners of this concept. And it's our ability to embrace vulnerability, to champion those who readily admit to their faults in a team setting, that allows us to learn constantly and field teams that consistently win.

BEHAVE THE WAY YOU WANT YOUR TEAM TO FOLLOW

The only way we're going to get our teammates to buy in to the notion that failure is more positive than negative and is therefore our mechanism to improved performance is to model the behaviors we want them to adopt. We must practice what we preach. We must:

Learn to be vulnerable in front of our peers and subordinates.

Reward those who follow our lead.

Frame our discussions in a way that highlights the positive aspects of failure, rather than the negative.

Yes, leadership is situational. Yes, there are times we'll use a different approach. And no, not all failures are good. We must enforce standards, and we need to remove people from their jobs when they can't get where they need to be. But those are the easy things for us to do. The concept we are sharing here is much more difficult—and therefore offers us greater reward when it's done well.

EMBRACE FAILURE.

POINTS TO PONDER

3.1   What emotions does failure spark in you?

3.2   What does psychological safety mean to you?

3.3   How can you better embrace failure?

CHAPTER 4

HUMANS IN THE LOOP

Perspective & Insight of
Daniel Walker

T he soft underbelly of every organization in their quest to be effective is the challenge of retaining and developing talent. There exists a myriad of barriers between achieving optimal levels of retention and striving for peak development. Far from the least of these challenges is the much talked about fact that there are more generations at work in the same companies than ever in human history. People who were born well before personal computing existed are working alongside and leading people who have never known a world without the most powerful computers ever produced. While this can be a problem, it doesn't have to remain one. To be successful, we must first focus on the most powerful and dynamic computing device, the humans in the loop.

WHY TALENT RETENTION MATTERS

The most effective way to maintain corporate knowledge is to retain the talented members who have accrued it over the course of advancing and growing the company. Their knowledge bears immeasurable value and can be hard to replace depending on continuity systems or the manner in which each person departed. Retention is not just about loss prevention. If a company can retain its best talent for long enough, it can evolve them into leaders of the next generation of workers, leaders who have grown into their roles as active members of an organization and ones who have the advantage of intimate knowledge of the organization. The advantage is mutual in that the home-grown leader knows how to navigate and shape the organization, while the entity benefits from the shaping and leading from someone who knows it best. While developing leaders from your most talented members is simple, it is never easy. An organization must ensure talented members learn the right lessons, share those lessons far and wide, and apply those lessons to create positive change. Although a simple formula, it is far easier said than done!

THE OLD AND YOUNG CAN BENEFIT EACH OTHER... WHO KNEW?

Another challenge to talent management is found in the generational gap. The gap is problematic because retaining and developing an organization's young talent is often done by its more senior leaders, who can vary widely in age and kinds of experiences. Though there may be a temptation here to break every generation down by its poor taste in music and coping strategies, I will instead focus on what we all have in common. From the most senior member of an organization to its newest, we were all young once. And in our youth, we all faced the most dreadful question of all: "What the heck am I going to do with my life?!"

Where generations differ, is how each answered and actioned on that question. My parents—each of whom are Baby Boomers—grew up, learned, and worked most of their lives in a culture of organizational loyalty. They chose an industry and a company, then committed to stick with each for the duration of their careers. My generation—the feared Millennials—watched as the financial crises of 2008 decimated our parents' finances and retirement plans. We responded with what some have coined 'Gig Culture.'

Millennials, and the generations after us, are like mercenaries who switch jobs and careers when the circumstances suit us. So, how are you supposed to retain us? By suggesting that the answer to the question of purpose is in the opportunities an organization can provide. To do that, address the root of the question itself.

Luckily, young people have wondered about purpose for as long as there have been young people. Because of the long and consistent history of existential crises, the bank of literature on the subject is vast; it turns out there has never been a shortage of youthful angst. My favorite description of the young person's dilemma comes from the *Bell Jar* by Sylvia Plath. In her novel, the antagonist, Esther, utters her famous allegory of the fig tree. For those of you who hate English Literature, feel free to take a quick nap. For the rest of you, the story goes like this:

"I saw my life branching out before me like the green fig tree in the story. From the tip of every branch, like a fat purple fig, a wonderful future beckoned and winked. One fig was a husband and a happy home and children, and another fig was a famous poet, and another fig was a brilliant professor, and another fig was Ee Gee, the amazing editor, and another fig was Europe and Africa and South America, and another fig was Constantin and Socrates and Attila and a pack of other lovers with queer names and offbeat professions, and another fig was an Olympic lady crew champion, and beyond and above these figs were many more figs I couldn't quite make out. I saw myself sitting in the crotch of this fig tree, starving to death, just because I couldn't make up my mind which of the figs I would choose. I wanted each and every one of them, but choosing one meant losing all the rest, and, as I sat there, unable to decide, the figs began to wrinkle and go black, and, one by one, they plopped to the ground at my feet."

"

Indecision is a decision.

Welcome back literature haters! During your nap you missed Esther so frozen in her indecisiveness that she watched in horror as the many life choices ahead of her—represented as frayed branches of a fig tree—withered up and died. She learned that indecision is a decision. This is the paradox of youth; in this situation each of us were young enough to have more options than one can choose, too young to know which one is right, but wise enough to know you can't choose them all.

A lot of young people entering the work force can relate, and as one of the most quoted allegories in modern literature, they are not alone in their struggle. However, there is a bit of a twist to this parable. It comes from the same novel, on the very next page. After sitting down to eat, "[Esther] felt immensely better after the first mouthful. It occurred to [her] that [her] vision of the fig tree and all the fat figs that withered and fell to earth might well have arisen from the profound void of an empty stomach."

Esther was hangry. That's it. She was freaking out about her future because she hadn't eaten yet. And that is the tragedy of youth; we don't quite appreciate all those calories our metabolisms are burning. The lesson we should take from Esther's growling stomach is that the future is serious business, but so are immediate actions and self-care. Sometimes we can get so lost looking at all the fig branches, that we forget that the most important parts of the tree are beneath us; the roots and the soil they rest in. Young, talented individuals are best served nurturing their growth from the bottom up. Organizations that want to recruit, develop, and retain that talent are best served in helping them do the nurturing. When young talent and organizations understand these truths, they can coexist productively, regardless of the generation gaps that exist.

AGE AND EXPERIENCE AS TOOLS FOR MENTORSHIP

When I mentor up and coming military officers, graduates, and family, I break all their choices down to the most granular and immediate actions. Sometimes, I am initially met with eye-rolls until we get to the actionable part of my stump speech where we decide, together, what must be done the following Monday. We then draw a clear line to how that task will inform their future decisions, thereby making their choices much more manageable. My mentee and I are, at that point, only concerned about Monday and not the whole of their professional existence. They also have a greater faith in that 'Monday' meaning something, namely progress. It's a Monday that moves them toward clarity, though they may not know exactly what is being clarified. This allows people of any age to accept a bit of uncertainty in their lives because they understand that though they may not have every answer, they are actively working toward finding them. They don't have to choose a fig branch right now; they just have to water the tree. And as their metaphorical tree grows, they'll gain intimate knowledge of the branches, making a choice between them much easier.

All of this is to say that those of us born before cell phones have the duty to help the Tik-Tokkers in our workforce explore themselves personally and professionally if we want them to stick around. Every one of us needs detailed guidance, but this up-and-coming generation has more choices at their fingertips at age eighteen than most of us have ever had or ever will have. While daunting, if an organization can accept this struggle, rather than fight against it, and embrace it by making life's choices more manageable through quality mentorship, then it can shift its young workforce's mindset from that of the gig to one of productive loyalty. As a result, the newly established, long-term collaboration between the organization and its young talent will net resolute corporate knowledge and a well-informed leadership structure ready to navigate the entity through an ever-dynamic future.

POINTS TO PONDER

4.1   What does this mean to you: "While developing leaders from your most talented members is simple, it is never easy."

4.2   How do you water your tree?

4.3   How can we positively embrace the generational gap?

CHAPTER 5

BE INTERESTED

Perspective & Insight of
Jason Harris

Often, upon entering a new organization, we are faced with the daunting task of figuring out what our role is and who we will become within the organization, on a particular team, and within the confines of our titled role. Even as I sit at my desk, pen to paper, and capture these thoughts, I am reminded how much these words are meant for me at this specific moment in my life and in my development.

This month I am embarking on a new journey with the challenge of taking the lead role of squadron commander one of the Air Force's newest Boeing KC-46 Tanker Squadrons. With this position, I will have both the honor and responsibility

"

Strive to be the most interested person, not the most interesting person.

of commanding airmen I have never flown with or even met in person before assuming this command. In this moment, I am reminded of the wisdom provided to me by one of my military aviation mentors on what it takes to step into a new organization and into the critical responsibility of leadership. How we enter in a new organization will determine how our team will view, perceive and receive us.

Any number of us have been guilty of entering an organization with the desire to be the popular person or even to be perceived as interesting by our fellow team members. You know the type, someone that everyone wants to know and hang out with. The reality is that when we enter an organization, no matter what our role and titles are, we should strive to be the most interested person, not the most interesting person.

Being the most interested person, interested in learning about our team members, allows us to build the foundations of trust. You start building this trust by communicating with team members and learning their unique stories that allows you to get to know people. As we get to know each other, we then begin to collectively know, like, trust and respect each other. This process all starts with being interested in others, taking the initiative and being intentional about getting to know the people around us.

Strive to be the most interested person in your environment. If we are interested in others, we create ample opportunity to get to know them. We can ask questions and learn about their backgrounds, work history, and perhaps even family dynamics, all of the elements that impact how we each show up every single day. Ultimately, being interested in others and getting to know them beyond their name and title allows us to find common ground with each other. When we find common ground, we can begin to move beyond the basics of knowing people.

Once we get to know each other, we move past the phase of merely knowing each other to perhaps respecting one another. It is important to acknowledge that it is not necessary that we like or respect every aspect of our peers on a personal level. Rather, as we get to know them, we realize the qualities that are most valuable in the context of our work, our organization, and our team(s). We learn to appreciate their traits that contribute to the job at hand. And often, we find that we have common ground that extends beyond the confines of the workplace.

Too often I have witnessed a new person enter an organization and lead with their resume, proclaiming their list of accolades and anything that might elevate them as an interesting person. Many times, their efforts are quite possibly made in an effort to create an affinity toward them. In the workplace, our nature is to tolerate these kinds of people and behaviors, but rarely do we trust them. Instead, their efforts are usually interpreted as self-serving, egotistical, and narcissistic. Being a leader requires us to be selfless, to care for our people, and to build trust. We cannot build a foundation of trust when people are only tolerating us. Rather, we must invest ourselves in getting to know, liking, trusting and respecting each other.

Once we get to know people and relationships advance, trust can be established. Trust is not automatic; it requires work and intentional action by those seeking trust. As people get to know us, we can begin to prove that we can be trusted. All too often, people want us to blindly trust them. Sure, we might work together, and we might even be in charge of some people that we work with, but that does not automatically constitute a relationship built on trust. It is important to note that as we enter and exist within organizations, our every action dictates whether we are destroying or building trust.

Building trust as a foundation to connect with those we are fortunate to work with has so many benefits. As we get to know people and build a level of trust, we begin to understand them. As we begin to understand them, we begin to appreciate them, as they are, for who they are and the great qualities they possess. We also gain a genuine appreciation for their background, lived experiences, and the unique talents they bring to the organization.

As we continue to work toward being an interested person, we find that is it indeed enjoyable and we learn that people enjoy being asked about themselves. People enjoy telling you all about who they are. People enjoy knowing that somebody, that we, truly care. And as we're doing this, we find that people absolutely love being provided an opportunity to share who they are. Fundamentally, being interested in others serves an innate human need and desire to be heard, understood, and acknowledged.

The concept of being interested in others extends beyond our peers. It is applicable to the people we work for, our peers, our team members, and those who might work for us. Across the spectrum, consider that we can create an atmosphere that breeds and cultivates trust, all based on being interested. Consider how being interested in those around you, hearing them, understanding them, and acknowledging them actually makes them feel. It's much like what Maya Angelou said, "People will forget what you said, people will forget what you did, but people will never forget how you made them feel."

It is important to understand and appreciate the power of how people feel when it comes to leadership. Imagine how you feel when someone takes an interest in you and begins to learn about you, your background, your goals, and your 'why'. Now consider how this makes those around you feel when you apply this same concept. When we spend time acknowledging who our people are and what our people want to accomplish, people begin to appreciate that we care. Studies show that when people know we care, they begin to change the dynamic of how they operate. Their appreciation for a leader who cares builds, and trust is cultivated, which leads to a culture of commitment to each other and to the mission.

What will you do today, tomorrow, and in the future that will enable you to cultivate trust? Will you choose to be the most interesting person or will you choose to be the most interested person? People are ready to share their story with you and waiting on you to ask. People are willing to be known. They are open to mutually getting to know, like, trust and respect each other.

POINTS TO PONDER

5.1   Are you the most interesting or the most inter-
        ested person on your team?

5.2   How do you feel when someone around you
        takes a genuine interest in you?

5.3   What will you do today, tomorrow, and in the
        future that will empower you to cultivate trust?

CHAPTER 6

LIVING HONORABLY

*Perspective & Insight of
Kim Campbell*

I t takes courage to give honest feedback and to hold both ourselves and others accountable. Most of us aren't good at it because it's uncomfortable. We would much prefer to be liked, to give positive feedback, and to let our team know when they've done well. But if we're only talking about the positive side of things, how do we ensure we're performing at the highest level? How do we ensure we are cultivating an environment in which our team can truly excel? A life lived in the world of high-performance teams says we have to demonstrate and encourage honesty, courage, and accountability at all levels of the organization in order to be our very best.

LEARNING BY EXAMPLE

"Hog 1, push it up. You're getting slow."

Those excruciating words echoed over the radio in the cockpit of my A-10 Warthog, an aircraft designed to fly low to the ground in order to support friendly forces. I was being evaluated while airborne on my ability to lead my four-ship of A-10s while conducting training to support our troops on the ground. At the time, I was making a critical mistake and my instructor was letting me know I wasn't meeting expectations. Unfortunately, I allowed my entire four-ship of A-10s to get too slow and too low--dangerous circumstances in flight--while we were waiting to attack the target. My instructor was giving me quick feedback, along with an opportunity to improve. Unfortunately, I couldn't quite recover from my mistake.

In our post-mission debrief, now safely back on the ground, I received even more feedback about the flight. Flying too low and too slow in the A-10 can be deadly. To lead a four-ship of A-10s, I had to do better. My instructor told me what I had done wrong, why it was wrong, and then provided techniques to fix the problem. The instruction wasn't personal; it was necessary feedback designed and delivered to make me better and to make the team better. My instructor could have just brushed it aside, but then where would that leave me as flight lead when it really mattered? As a result of my shortfalls on the flight, my grade sheet was covered with red marks and critiques of what I had done wrong. My instructor understood that his responsibility was to make the tough call, to give me the feedback I needed to improve. Ultimately, he made me do that portion of the ride again, an outcome that stung. However, even in the midst of the tough feedback, my instructor also highlighted the good, reinforcing the things I did well on the ride. It gave me confidence to go out and do it again, this time meeting expectations.

In the world of fighter aircraft, we must operate as a high performing team because lives are on the line. We rely on honesty, courage, and accountability to ensure individuals, and therefore teams, perform at their absolute best when the situation demands it. This doesn't just apply to fighter pilots. In the business world, livelihoods are on the line. A business needs to survive in order to provide paychecks and benefits to its employees. The principles are the same—winning teams require honesty, courage, and accountability.

A few short months after this training mission, I would have the honor and responsibility to lead a four-ship of A-10s on a combat mission in Afghanistan. The weather was terrible, and the terrain was dangerous, but we had the critical mission of supporting our troops on the ground. I could not afford to make the same mistake of getting too low or too slow. Thankfully, my instructor had the courage to hold me accountable, to do what was right, even if it meant giving me some undesirable feedback. As a result, I learned from that failure, and we achieved mission success and lived to tell the tale.

LEADING BY EXAMPLE

The lessons and skills I learned operating in high performing fighter squadrons also translates to my experience as a commander and leader of people. Eleven years after my experience in Afghanistan, I would take command of the 612th Theater Operations Group and the 474th Air Expeditionary Group. My airmen were spread overseas from South America and Central America to the Caribbean. Now, instead of leading a four-ship of A-10s, I was responsible for more than 1,500 personnel at the peak of operations. The missions performed by my organization varied from counterdrug operations to humanitarian assistance and disaster relief missions to detention operations.

My team of squadron commanders—my direct reports—were deployed throughout the region and responsible for their team and mission sets. For many, this was their first real-world leadership opportunity. They needed help managing and leading their teams, as most new leaders do. As their boss, I owed it to them to provide feedback they needed to help them improve. Personally, I dreaded some of those conversations.

Leaders tend to enjoy doing what we perceive as 'good' things: we love celebrating promotions, giving people time off, awards, or congratulatory announcements—the accolades most of our teammates enjoy receiving. The more challenging side of leadership is letting people know when they have missed the mark. It's much harder to advise a teammate that we can't recommend them for promotion or that they need to

A good leader is willing
to do the right thing even
when it's hard.

rethink their leadership approach. Those conversations aren't fun; they're not an enjoyable part of the job—and yet we owe it to our teammates to have the courage to make those tough calls. It's our duty to have difficult conversations.

A good leader is willing to do the right thing even when it's hard. It's not easy and, speaking personally, it is by far my least favorite aspect of leading a team. However, we owe it to our teammates to act with integrity and to hold them—and ourselves—accountable. By holding difficult conversations for the right reasons and delivering them in the right way, we actually help our team excel in the long run. If, on the other hand, we let the mistakes continue simply because we're afraid to have a hard conversation, then we do a grave disservice to our team.

To truly be effective, we must first create an environment of trust with our team in which they will not feel blame or shame. We do that by being honest and transparent with our team. However, these conversations are not just about sharing negative feedback and situations we need to improve; they're also about offering positive reinforcement and encouraging behaviors we want our team to continue. As a commander, I learned to apply what my A-10 instructor demonstrated through his actions—I had to have the courage to honestly hold my team accountable even though it was tough to do.

A LEADER OF CHARACTER

In July of 2020, I became the Director for the Center for Character and Leadership Development at the United States Air Force Academy. The Academy's mission is to develop officers of character, motivated to lead the Air Forces and Space Forces in service to the nation. The Academy's Center for Character and Leadership Development designed a framework that defined a leader of character. This framework explains how the institution will approach developing such leaders based on research and collaboration with experts. A leader of character is defined as someone who lives honorably, lifts others to their best possible selves, and elevates performance toward a common and noble purpose. The framework provides leaders with a focus on their own development as well as that of their teammates.

Living honorably is about consistently practicing virtues like honesty, courage, and accountability. It doesn't mean we're perfect or we don't make mistakes. A leader of character is someone who is constantly working to improve, to be better, to live up to their virtues and ideals. And when we fall short of our virtues, then we figure out how to do it better the next time. Becoming a leader of character who lives honorably is a journey, one filled with constant learning and improvement. Living honorably requires regular, even ritualized, reflection. We must examine who we are, how we align with key virtues, how we see ourselves, and how we contribute to the larger mission in our organization.

When we live honorably, we consistently practice honesty and evaluate our performance based on set standards. We work hard to improve based on our own merit. And we act with courage, even when we're afraid. Living honorably requires action in the face of fear. We need to exercise the courage to make tough calls and initiate difficult conversations. We hold ourselves accountable by admitting mistakes, being transparent, and seeking honest and constructive feedback.

If we are going to be a leader of character who lives honorably, then we have to model correct behavior for our team. We must be willing to let our team know when it's time to 'push it up'. I'm extremely thankful my A-10 instructor taught me this valuable lesson so early in my career—that honesty, courage, and accountability matter, that you can teach a tough lesson in a positive way, and that living honorably creates trust in an organization and empowers a team to perform at their very best.

POINTS TO PONDER

6.1   As a leader, it's your duty to have difficult conversations with your team. How do you structure these interactions to ensure they are conducted in a team-building fashion?

6.2   To truly be effective, a leader must first create an environment of trust with their team in which they will not feel blame or shame. How do you ensure this construct on your team?

6.3   A leader of character is defined as someone who lives honorably, lifts others to their best possible selves, and elevates performance toward a common and noble purpose. How do you ensure you are a leader of character?

CHAPTER 7

CREATING TRUST

Perspective & Insight of
Jason Harris

P eople are simple. Everyone wants to be heard, understood, and acknowledged. They want to be heard, when they speak, understood when they share information, and acknowledged when they have concerns. The key to affording people the opportunity to be heard, understood, and acknowledged (HUA) is to engender an environment of psychological safety. Beyond this, leaders must build and cultivate trust based on actions, not just words.

HEARD, UNDERSTOOD, & ACKNOWLEDGED

People need to know they are valued. An easy way for us, as leaders, to show people they are valued is to engage three basic elements of good communication. We must show, more than just tell, that we hear, understand, and acknowledge our people. By doing so, we demonstrate that we value them and their input.

Let me be clear. In no way do I think leaders can fix, solve, and address every single problem that is brought to us in the workplace. The same is true when leading in our homes. Leaders must learn to set aside their pride and ego and admit they are unable to solve and fix everything that is thrown their way. That said, leaders should commit to hearing the problems and challenges of their team. They must be willing and able to understand the challenges presented to them. And leaders must do their best to acknowledge what is brought to their attention.

It is imperative that our people know we hear them first and foremost. This is critical as leaders, mentors, supervisors, and peers. People are often hurting and want to know they will be heard in their most vulnerable times. When we truly listen, we confirm that we will be there for them no matter the circumstance.

Our people need to next know we understand them. At best, we need to first hear, then understand what our people are going through. This applies to race, gender, generational challenges, and many other issues we are faced with in the workplace. Understanding doesn't mean you need a PhD in what someone is experiencing; it simply means you are willing to listen and learn. Those concepts alone can make a world of a difference for a person who is experiencing a genuine challenge, whether simple or complex.

Once you hear and understand, the next logical step is to acknowledge the person's presence, feelings, and challenges in their given situation. Acknowledging, after hearing and understanding, what someone might be dealing with allows us as leaders to express empathy. Empathy is a powerful tool that demonstrates we sincerely care and value our people.

Everyone longs to feel included and supported in the workplace. When people feel they have been included by way of being heard, understood, and acknowledged, it impacts productivity and the overall success of the organization in a positive way. A sense of support and inclusion leads to a sense of empowerment that translates into improved performance, according to a Salesforce Special Report (2017). The report also reveals that employees are 4.6 times more likely to feel empowered to perform at their best when they feel like they are heard.

As you set out to be a leader, with or without a title, in your organization and in life, never be too busy to stop, look, and listen to what people have to say. Taking a small amount of time to look someone in the eye and let them know they have been heard, understood, and acknowledged will make a huge difference in how they view themselves and how they view you as a leader. This seemingly simple act cultivates trust with people around you and each one of your team members.

PSYCHOLOGICAL SAFETY

Psychological safety is defined by the Center for Creative Leadership as the belief that speaking up with ideas, questions, concerns, or mistakes will not be punished or met with punitive repercussions. According to Harvard Business Review (HBR), the highest performing teams have one thing in common: psychological safety. As we lead, it is imperative to cultivate a culture that values psychological safety, allowing each person to be heard, understood, and acknowledged without fear of repercussions or retribution.

I recall what it felt like being a newly minted pilot with a fresh set of wings that had barely settled onto my uniform. I had gone through a grueling year of pilot training, and it seemed that the only way we were instructed and taught how to fly was by way of fear, sarcasm, and ridicule. I felt as though my opinion and perspective didn't matter. I began to feel uncomfortable speaking up. I did not feel like my voice would be heard or acknowledged if I offered input. I began to shut down and stopped contributing my perspective. I did not feel psychologically safe.

It wasn't until an (old, crusty) senior officer held an impromptu mentor session with me and several other newly minted pilots that I considered sharing my thoughts. He invited us to speak up and offer our perspectives and input on the day's training mission. He informed us that our input mattered and was valued. He encouraged us that it was our duty to be a beacon for change by way of ensuring that each voice on our flight crews and in our squadrons were heard and valued. This senior officer single-handedly created a significant amount of psychological safety, in just one conversation. Ultimately, this old, crusty senior officer was advising us to create and cultivate a culture of psychological safety in an effort to create the highest performing flight crews.

When we create an environment with psychological safety as its foundation, people are empowered to speak up without fear of reprisal or ostracization. This is critical to an organization's success. Psychological safety sets in motion a framework in which people will feel valued. When people feel valued, they become more committed. Working with individuals who are committed to each other and the organization is how we build trust!

BUILD & CULTIVATE TRUST BASED ON ACTIONS

It is vital that we not only tell our people they are valued, but that we show them. We exhibit this by genuinely caring for and paying attention to our people. Of course, this starts with hearing, understanding, and acknowledging through our actions hand in hand with consciously creating psychological safety. When people do not feel as though they are valued, they will respond in kind, with the same lack of commitment they are being shown. This leads to decreased productivity. Further, people who feel undervalued or devalued respond by leaving the organization. For these reasons, it is imperative that we build trust with deliberate actions beyond our words.

Trust in an organization

is a precious commodity.

Trust in an organization is a precious commodity. It is hard to earn and easy to lose. The actions of a leader in an organization determine how trust is earned, maintained, or lost. In a study conducted by Washington University in St. Louis and State University of New York, it was revealed that positive impacts toward commitment in an organization, job performance, or overall job satisfaction is based on an individual's trust in the leadership. Additionally, a Harvard Business Review article suggested that a leader's trustworthiness is evaluated based on competence, motives, means, and impact. Ultimately, leadership is evaluated based on actions.

As leaders, we must generate an intentional plan that demonstrates to our people that they are valued which leads to cultivating commitment, accountability and trust.. We must be mindful in how we show people, from the janitor to the CEO, that they are valued, trusted, heard, and empowered to be their best selves every single day. This is not an easy task, as each of us have our own unique personalities and challenges we are faced with every day.

I recall being a member of an organization early in my career where I, along with others, did not feel valued. I personally felt like my contributions were not valued and what I was doing was not appreciated by my leadership. After a while, I began to become uninterested in giving more effort, energy and support to the mission and daily tasks. I began to feel ignored. I consciously chose to stop sharing ideas and input. I looked around and realized that others were beginning to take the same approach as many of them felt unvalued. This was catastrophic to the organizations morale and minimized our overall mission effectiveness. I along with others began to check out mentally, and some began to check out physically. As leaders, we must recognize when people stop talking because they don't feel valued, they start leaving, mentally and physically. If you want people to be accountable and committed, it is essential they feel like they are valued and able to make meaningful contributions to an organization.

Leading people is hard, yet a rather simple task. The key elements are summed up by way of communication skills, psychological safety, and deliberate actions. Although this sounds quite easy to implement, many organizations and individuals in leadership roles struggle to do so due to a lack of quality communication, psychological safety, and inaction.

Start today being deliberate in your actions as a leader, whether you have a title or not. Be conscious to hear, seek to understand, and acknowledge those around you. Create and cultivate spaces of psychological safety. Be deliberate in your actions, ensuring you are competent, moved by the right motives and means, and making a positive impact. You will then lead people, an organization, and an environment built on trust.

POINTS TO PONDER

7.1   What does empathy mean to you? And how do you lead with empathy?

7.2   A leader's trustworthiness is evaluated on competence, motives, means, and impact. Ultimately, leadership is evaluated based on actions. How do you build proper trustworthiness in your organization?

7.3   How do you, as a leader, create a deliberate plan to show people they are valued?

CHAPTER 8

LESSONS FROM CORPORATE AMERICA

Perspective & Insight of
Chris Stricklin

Today, I started off by smelling a full moon on a crisp Manhattan evening. Next, I smelled a red-tailed hawk in-flight. Yesterday, I would not have believed it possible to envision these pictures in my mind, generated with eyes closed while holding a test tube under my nose in a laboratory. But today, the passionate gentleman standing in front of me created them through chemistry, experience, and artistry. His name is Ron Winnegrad. He teaches the art of fragrance, or synesthesia. He pioneered a synesthetic approach that enables one to understand scents through multiple senses.

Opening with those two unbelievable, but 100% true, events is the only way I can think to free your mind enough to fathom the revelations revealed to me over an amazing 48-hour period. On the heels of my recent retirement from the military, I jumped into the deep end of the business world with both feet. A valued mentor called me into his office one day and offered the opportunity to build my business acumen faster than I could ever have imagined by shadowing Andreas Fibig, International Flavors & Fragrances CEO and leader of a 100+ year-old multi-national $37B+ company. Never in my wildest dreams did I imagine the knowledge, skill, and corporate success secrets that would be revealed to me from the leadership team of International Flavors & Fragrances (IFF). Money could not buy and college could not instill the corporate success and insights I experienced in an amazingly insightful 48 hours with Andreas and his elite team. In one short visit I found a way to translate what I knew as a combat-proven leader into the business world by way of seeing it unfold before my eyes at IFF.

As I boarded the flight back to Alabama from Manhattan, I felt guilty for the amount of knowledge I had been freely given. I would be remiss if I did not share these ten brilliant and insightful lessons from the IFF C-Suite. Whether leading 1,000 soldiers in combat or 7,000 people in corporate America, leadership is a universal skill set. Armed with the following 10 simple lessons, you will improve your chances for success in your role as a follower, a leader, and as an individual in general.

Whether leading 1,000

soldiers in combat or

7,000 people in corporate

America, leadership is a

universal skill set.

1. SUCCESSION

On your first day on the job, in any job, create a succession folder. I know you feel like you just arrived and don't have any plans to leave your company but trust me—plan for your departure from the beginning. Do so to set your eventual successor up for a better start than you had, with both the lessons and the secrets you will learn each day the hard way. This is a simple way to prove to your team you care about company success and not just individual progress.

2. PLAN FOR CONTINGENCIES

Andreas shared that most people think the hardest part of being a CEO is developing a master plan for success. His contention is that the CEO's role is MUCH more. Andreas impressed upon me that a successful CEO's vision must include actionable, deliberate, detailed back-up plans. The geo-political aspects of international business, which every business is to some degree in the flattened world of today, are what will break a CEO, executive team, or company entirely if not given the necessary attention.

With a concerned expression, he leaned forward in his chair and delivered an anecdote he knew I would understand, as a former fighter pilot. He proceeded to share that his most stressful day in the C-Suite was when a Turkish F-16 downed a Russian Su-24. He explained that his company has a manufacturing plant in Turkey that exports products to Russia. Shaking his head, he detailed his worry for his customers. As political tensions escalated, there was a potential of borders closing and deliveries being delayed. As a business-to-business supplier, this would not only hurt the credibility of his company but also the reputations of those companies in the chain who relied on timely deliveries for theirs. As a company with production facilities in over 30 countries, he immediately increased production at another factory, at a significantly greater cost of both production and shipping, to mitigate the possible problem before it manifested into one.

Enterprise Risk Management, he revealed, was his biggest challenge. As a truly global firm with customers in 100+ countries and production in 30+ countries, his executive team is required to continually strive to forecast where the supply chain could be interrupted and how the company will react. For every new factory opened, there is a plan of action to address location shut down for an hour, a week, or eternity. They prepare for the worst so that they can remain the best.

3. SERVE ON CORPORATE BOARDS

As Jim Rohn pointed out, "You are the average of the five people you spend time with." With this, Andreas detailed the importance of serving on corporate boards, albeit never those of customers or competitors. Serving on a corporate board is, in Andreas' estimation, an opportunity to share best practices, network, benchmark, and cross-communicate. He explained recently that a peer needed to raise venture capital, so he sent his VC expert over to help. Months later when Andreas was exploring ways to grow in a new country, his friend returned the favor by sending his country expert over to assist. In all cases, we must grow the community of practice and leave a better industry and society as our legacy. Remember, a rising tide lifts all boats.

4. SET STRATEGY & APPLY ABSTRACT ALLOCATION OF CAPITAL

A CEO has only two duties: set strategy for the organization and allocate capital to enable success. That's it. This individual must be visionary as they look to build future success from today's facts. And capital allocation spans all available company resources, from money and people to time and effort. If the properly skilled and motivated individuals have been placed in the correct seats, they will take care of execution. Empower them to make decisions at the appropriate level. Trust them to act in the best interests of the company and know when to elevate a decision that is above their risk acceptance or strategic level. Empower people to say no, but also trust them to say yes.

5. NURTURE RELATIONSHIPS

As a global organization, the question of in-person or in-technology always arises. Recognize that every meeting is an opportunity, a unique moment that can bring a team closer together or shred the fabric that binds them. Many leaders talk about developing teams, but few truly understand the complexities and intricacies of establishing the necessary culture of unity.

The key to success reaffirmed in my visit to IFF was to always hold initial meetings face-to-face, to understand each other personally, and build the foundation of a strong and trusting relationship. Only after that has been accomplished is video conferencing acceptable. Minimize purely voice communications because neither side can read body language nor emotion.

Andreas shared that one of his executive team lives on the other side of the world. Because of this, IFF invested in a robot. The robot consists of a rolling base with a video screen and a camera. In the beginning, this robot version of the executive is present in meetings like all the other members of the staff. This means neither side misses a hand gesture or emotional response. It is as if they are together, face-to-face. While he initially was hesitant to embrace technology to replicate the absent team member, Andreas now finds the robot to be an outstanding asset…because it works. Remember: Each relationship with each member of a successful team requires proper care and feeding.

6. BE TRANSPARENT

One of IFF's Chief of Staff's jobs is to build the shell of the CEOs calendar for the next year. This shell includes scheduled time with customers, investors, employees, manufacturing plants, town halls, business reviews, and vacations. This shell is sent to literally everyone at IFF. As a result, there are no secrets as to how the CEO spends his time. IFF has total Time Transparency. Everyone is important enough to know how their CEO works, when he vacations, and where he travels. The first year, many asked Andreas' Chief of Staff, Michael DeVeau, why? The next year they understood and instead replied with their own 12-month schedules. The result was a more deliberate organization with effective and efficient allocation of time, as the VPs and other executives began complimenting the CEO's trips and meetings with their own. The Company's efforts were more aligned. The team was executing as one.

7. ATTENTION EQUALS RETENTION

Managing the Talent Agenda is a continuous effort. I heard this message loud and clear from Andreas, as well as from his EVP & Chief Human Resources, Diversity, and Inclusion Officer, Doctor Susana Suarez-Gonzalez. They were living what Jim Collins informed us—that it is just as important to get the right people on the bus and in the right seat as it is to get the wrong people off the bus. Have the guts to act when people do not meet expectations or perform at the required level. This will reaffirm to your high performers that they are members of an elite team. The true competitive advantage in any industry is found in the team, not the product. People, not things. Talent, not trademarks. True teamwork is about shared purpose, determined success, and vested interest.

Treat each member of the team like they are your most important customer. Give them your full attention when interacting with them. Don't just hear what they are saying, listen to what they mean. Know where they are on Maslow's hierarchy of needs. Never assume money is their only motivator. While many workers may be incentivized by pay increases in the basic needs section of the pyramid, many others in today's world are more motivated by self-actualization desires. They need only for you to listen, to hear them, and to acknowledge they are not only special but critical to organizational success. A young parent may value time with their infant and new spouse over a pay increase. A mid-level leader may want to improve their knowledge through professional classes. And a senior team member may value spending time volunteering to work on a legacy project. Know if an individual is motivated by money, acknowledgement, or success, and, if success, is it organizational or individual? Do you know what motivates each member of your team? Do you push each level of leadership to know their team in this manner? Many times, people need to know how they made a difference and that what they have devoted their lives to matters.

8. ENSURE EACH MEMBER KNOWS HOW CRITICAL THEY ARE TO SUCCESS

In IFF's multi-national market, everyone shuts down over Christmas. Andreas directs all staff to go home, spend time with their families and not come back to work until after the holidays. On Christmas Eve, a member of the executive team stopped by the office to pick up some files she needed. As she entered the elevator, the man tasked with mailing samples to prospective customers was stepping off, carrying large boxes. Intrigued, she queried what he was doing on this day, one in which no one was supposed to be at work. He replied, "If I do not get this in the mail, we will not succeed as a company!" In the discussion that followed, he revealed that all three of IFF's major competitors were shut down for the holiday the same as IFF. Since he was tasked with sending samples, he came in to do it on this day to ensure his company's samples were shipped and would be waiting at the customer's office when they returned from their own holidays. This would ensure his company was afforded first look, first examination, before all the competitors. He beamed with pride as he revealed his confidence in this strategy and how he was vital to success. He was not merely an employee; it was his company. And he knew how vital he was to its success.

As a leader, do your employees work for you or with you? To be a successful leader, you must not only inspire others with confidence in you but, more importantly, inspire them with confidence in themselves. Give credit where credit is due and instill in the team an intrinsic pride and ownership which will propel your organization to heights previously thought unachievable.

9. SIMPLICITY ELEGANCY

Many people in today's world wear their task load like a badge of honor. They are proud of the complexity of the emergencies they handled this week, the number of emails they turned, and the outrageous number of hours they logged in the office. Yet the art of success is found in simplifying the complex. Allow your team to task-shed responsibilities.

Remember, if everything is top priority, nothing is top priority. Simplify your organization by allowing smaller tasks to wait until next week. Simplify by prioritizing the important things required for your organizational success. While thinking on my time at IFF I found myself reflecting on my time as a junior officer at the Pentagon. I had the honor of working for a senior Air Force general who was the Air Force's first female wing commander, Major General Marne Peterson. One day we were working what seemed to be the most important task of my life. As we reached the unified frustration of not having a solution to a demanding problem, she picked up her gym bag. As I looked on in disbelief, she said, "Never sit there and beat your head against the wall. When you reach the point of no progress, take a break. Some of your greatest breakthroughs will happen on a relaxing run." We went for a 5-mile run and found the elusive solution to our problem as we rounded mile three. Glowing with that 'I told you so' pride, she continued, "If the boss can walk away and take a break, it gives everyone else permission to do the same."

10. NEVER FORGET TO CARE

My very first question of Andreas, behind closed doors, of course, was an aggressive one and was meant to set the tone for our time together: "Do you enjoy being CEO?" With the enthusiasm of a child on Christmas morning, he sprang to the front of his chair and, beaming with pride, proceeded to explain how amazing he found his company. From the positive impact his company has on the environment to the local improvements it regularly makes in each of the countries/communities in which it operates. From the success of the executive team to the pride of the chemist who makes their products, from the ownership of the deliveryman to the attention to detail of the person who runs the mixing robot producing their products. It was through this answer, or better yet through his manner of answering, he revealed the simple secret to becoming successful at any job. Never forget to care. Care for the people around you, the part of their lives they dedicate to the company, the environment/communities in which you operate, and the legacy you leave. The simple secret to becoming successful at any job is to never forget to care.

As President Roosevelt once said, "People do not care how much you know until they know how much you care!" As I reflect on my time at IFF, and specifically on this principle, I'm overcome with a sense of awe at the power of caring.

And so, as this article opened, it will also close with a reminder that whether leading 1,000 soldiers in combat or 7,000 people in corporate America, leadership is a universal skill set! Simply care about the people, care about the process, the success and succession. With these simple lessons, you will improve your chances for success in your role as a follower, a leader, and an individual.

Closing note: A sincere and personal thank you to Andreas Fibig and his amazing team at IFF! Your leadership is both insightful and inspiring. Thank you for helping a combat-proven military leader grow and expand his knowledge to be successful in the business arena! For your mentorship, I remain eternally grateful.

POINTS TO PONDER

8.1   Who is your most influential mentor, and how did he/she enable you to grow to the leader you are today?

8.2   How do you empower a team to make decisions at appropriate levels and build trust to a level that allows them to act in the best interests of the company?

8.3   Do you feel that leadership is a universal skill set? Why or why not.

CHAPTER 9

LIFTING OTHERS

Perspective & Insight of
Kim Campbell

think we can agree from the outset that leaders should be credible in order to be effective. To truly be effective at leading, they also need to empower their teammates to perform at their best. Leaders have a responsibility, a duty, to nurture the strengths and talents of those around us. Our role as leaders should be to lift others and to encourage our teammates to be their best possible selves.

A LEADER OF CHARACTER

I was blessed to finish my career leading the Center for Character and Leadership Development at the United States Air Force Academy. The Air Force Academy's Leader of Character Framework—a framework we teach future air and space leaders—defines a Leader of Character as someone who lives honorably, lifts others to their best possible selves, and elevates performance toward a common and noble purpose. When we lift others, we help them pursue the best of who they are and who they want to become. To do this effectively, leaders must first take the time to truly connect with their teammates, helping them to feel valued and understood. When we connect with the members of our team, we earn their trust. It is then and only then that we truly lift others to help them perform at their very best.

Leaders owe it to their team to provide guidance and support when they need it most. Leaders have a responsibility to identify and support the strengths of their teammates, with an equal responsibility to challenge, nurture, and mitigate weaknesses. Leaders ultimately have to respect the members of their team for who they are and what they bring to the table. It is our role to challenge our team to improve, to hold them accountable for executing their plans for improvement, and to continuously strive for excellence. We can help our teammates improve by encouraging them to get outside their comfort zones, try new ways of doing things, and find opportunities for meaningful and purposeful experiences.

LEARNING BY EXAMPLE

We've come to expect the standard of performance to be that everyone performs at their very best. To nurture this culture, we must make every effort to develop our team, to ensure they each have opportunities for meaningful and purposeful engagement.

One of the most meaningful and purposeful training experiences in fighter aviation is Red Flag. Red Flag is the Air Force's premier air-to-air combat simulation and provides aircrew the experience of multiple, intensive combat missions in the relative safety of a training environment. Perhaps the most important aspect of Red Flag is the simple fact that we all push each other to execute at the highest possible level—the expectation is that we each perform at our best. Most fighter pilots will tell you that the real learning at Red Flag happens after the mission is complete. It takes place in our post-mission debriefs, the place where we provide open, honest feedback and discuss learning points from the mission.

I recall a particular Red Flag mission, one where I was responsible for leading a four-ship of A-10s across the invisible but meaningful 'push line', crossing into what we were simulating as enemy territory. We descended low to merely 100 feet above the ground to avoid enemy threats by hiding behind the terrain, reducing the possibility of being detected by both enemy ground and air threats. By following our tactics, we were able to make it to the target area undetected. At the last possible moment, we rose above the terrain to deliver our rockets and bombs on the enemy compound. As we maneuvered out of the area post-attack, I could hear high-pitched tones in my helmet, telling me an enemy missile was tracking me. I maneuvered hard to get away from the threat while simultaneously dispensing chaff and flares, countermeasures used by military aircraft to help evade a missile attack. Diving back to just 100 feet above the rocky Nevada terrain in a last-ditch attempt to again hide from the enemy threat systems, I evaded the threat. My wingmen followed behind me, working hard to escape the enemy threat as well. Our understanding was that if we could do this effectively in training, then we would all be better prepared for combat when the stakes were highest.

We delivered our ordnance on target and made it home safely. The mission was a success. But like every mission, we had several learning points along the way—we are not flawless, and we are always looking for ways to improve. My real job as a leader was just beginning because it was my responsibility to lead the debrief. It was my responsibility to derive the key lessons learned for every member of my team. Based on the debrief, we learned a lot of lessons that day even in the midst of our success.

For an event or experience to be purposeful and meaningful, leaders must take the time to analyze and discuss how our missions are going. We must ask ourselves, what did we do well and where could we do better the next time. As the flight lead and mission commander, it was my responsibility to derive those key lessons learned and to provide feedback to my team. Did we meet our mission objectives? Where could we have done better in our execution? Did we accept more risk than we needed? Did we make errors we needed to fix? What was the reason for those errors? What were the critical learning points that we could take with us on the next mission? The requirement in the fighter pilot world is that each time we fly, we learn something new, and over time, we improve to levels of performance as the best in the world. Most importantly, we share those lessons learned with our team to lift them and help them perform at their best as well.

In the business world, we must use these same techniques to develop our teams and to help our teammates perform at their very best. Doing so allows us to provide meaningful development opportunities for our teammates. Negotiation complete . . . did we meet our objectives? Finished presenting to senior management . . . how did we do? What are the key learning points we can pull from these experiences and then share with others in order to enable our team to improve?

LEADING BY LIFTING OTHERS

When I took my most recent command—when I became the equivalent of a CEO—of a team of more than 1,500 employees, I took the time to get to know my team. I spent time walking around and talking with my new teammates, striving to connect with them so that I could help develop them. I wanted them to grow and learn and contribute to the organization. It certainly wasn't easy, and it took time to get out and walk around and talk to the members of my team. At each

As leaders, it is critical to make time to connect with our teammates so we can help them improve, to fight to be better, to become their best possible selves.

location I visited, I scheduled time to meet with each individual team in the organization. I talked to the least experienced members of these teams, just as I talked to the most experienced members. I wanted to learn from each of them. How were things going? What struggles were they facing?

I met with them in small groups, so they felt comfortable sharing their ideas. It took time for them to connect with me and to know I was truly listening, but it was worth the time and effort. I learned a lot from my teammates and developed a good sense of how the team was doing. Doing this allowed me to position myself to lift these important team members. By earning their trust and connecting with them, we developed in ways that supported the mission. We found ourselves more prepared as a team to face a crisis. When I asked my teammates to do hard things or things they didn't necessarily like, they trusted me, and they did what was required. They did so because I took time to explain my reasoning behind the tough decisions. As leaders, it is critical to make time to connect with our teammates so we can help them improve, to fight to be better, to become their best possible selves.

It was especially important that members of my extended executive leadership team were developing as leaders as well. To get their feedback and assess their performance, I conducted frequent visits to meet with them and their teams. I needed their feedback to really gain an understanding of how things were truly going in the organization. On one of these visits, I learned that one of the organizations was struggling with their senior leadership. The local CEO—we call them squadron commanders, responsible for about 150 people—just wasn't connecting with the team. The team members were especially frustrated with many of his policies. It was my responsibility to mentor him, to ensure he had the skills and abilities needed to lead his organization. We sat down together and talked through what was going on with his team. I challenged some of his assumptions, and I also encouraged him to think about new ways of doing things, to find ways to connect with his team. Most importantly, I supported him in his efforts. It was hard for him to hear he was not connecting with his team, and that he was not yet effective as a new leader. I thoughtfully suggested a few ideas and helped him to adapt and evolve his leadership style. Over time he improved, and his team responded positively. It was my responsibility to help him become his best possible self.

Lifting others to their best possible selves is a critical component to ensuring a team can perform at the highest level. As leaders, we have a responsibility to develop our people. We help our teammates perform at their best by connecting with them and providing meaningful and purposeful experiences. As a leader, we have a responsibility to train our replacements. We should train them to be better than us and teach them the things we wish we had learned earlier in our careers. We must be confident enough in ourselves to know we can develop them so that one day, they will outperform us. Performing this responsibility well, coupled with your own successes, will constitute a lasting legacy.

POINTS TO PONDER

9.1 How do you nurture the strengths of those around you?

9.2 Why is it important to explain the reasoning behind a decision when you could just tell your team what to do?

9.3 How do you ensure that you train them to be better than you and teach them the things you wish you had learned earlier in your career?

CHAPTER 10

HANDLING ADVERSITY

Perspective & Insight of
Robert Teschner

I n my life, there was a single tumultuous day that changed my life forever.

The doctor walked in with a heavy heart. The magnitude of his words, of his discovery, hit instantly. A life-changing jolt of adrenaline made the world freeze around me. The massive tumor in my lower colon was very likely cancer, potentially advanced cancer. The news was breath-taking.

The doctor was apologetic. His manner, words and overall demeanor spoke volumes: he was very worried for me and fearful for my family. This day went from upbeat and happy to shockingly horrible in an instant.

Still groggy from the anesthesia that preceded the colonoscopy, I recognized immediately that my world had been forever altered from this point forward. Sitting next to my beautifully pregnant wife on a bright sunny day in downtown Stuttgart, Germany, we realized at that moment we were now in for a fight for my life. The best case, if things went extremely well, was a long fight for my family. More importantly, we realized this was a fight I could also lose, and quickly. In the days that followed, tidal waves of challenges were forming in my mind and would overwhelm at random times. Our situation was decidedly not good and was rapidly deteriorating.

Looking back on that tumultuous day the only word that best articulates our demeanor in that exact moment was extreme calm.

My wife and I left the doctor's office and immediately went to lunch. I was famished from the colonoscopy prep and my wife, was starving as well, eating for two in the third month of her pregnancy. In stark contrast to the news we just received, it was a stunningly gorgeous day. I am always amazed at the specific detail one can remember from everything around them after receiving life-altering news. The sunshine was a welcome break from the dreary winter, a break which ultimately helped soothe our souls. We started to regroup as a team while sitting in a bright, cheerful café on the ground floor of the doctor's office. Lunch was remarkably peaceful.

We discussed our initial action steps and began crafting the outline of our near-term game plan. Time was not on our side as the tumor was massive; we recognized the bias for action that would be required in the days that followed. Upon this reflection here today, it turns out the process of building our plan helped us maintain our calm.

We recognized that moving forward we would need to make high-quality decisions often with incomplete facts. Simultaneously, we realized there was no way to know whether the decisions we would make would be correct until after we lived the results...a tough situation driven by the complexity of our circumstances. This realization, however, gave us peace in the midst of the storm. We were determined to make the best decisions possible with the situation presented and further resolved to adjust those decisions based on what we learned real-time.

OUR CORE APPROACH

Subconsciously, my Air Force training took over and I was driven by the mental model every pilot relies on in emergency situations and one immediately embraced by my wife after I shared it:

- Maintain aircraft control.

- Analyze the situation and take appropriate action.

- Land as soon as conditions permit.

These three lines define how pilots handle emergencies in the air. They are cemented into our brains early in pilot training, and we reference them constantly throughout our flying careers. The approach is centered on prioritizing tasks, learning to make smart decisions that help us solve the right problem the right way at the right time with the facts as they present in that moment. These lines are also a driver for taking action and, ultimately, outlining an approach organized to help us return home safely.

Consider this scenario: We're flying an F-15, a supersonic high-tech fighter aircraft, and while upside down, fighting in a dogfight against an adversary, we experience a master caution light with a corresponding engine fire light. This suggests we have an engine on fire—a situation that demands our immediate attention and the appropriate corrective action. The steps we take from the moment we realize we're dealing with an emergency define whether we'll come through the situation the right way. Immediately, we learn to do the following:

Maintain aircraft control. This is a reminder to prioritize flying—to make sure we don't hit a mountain or crash into the water or do something else that would jeopardize our ability to return home safely. Translated into the non-flying world, this means we focus on core tasks that keep things running while determining how to navigate the uncertainty of the moment. Think 'keep the lights on now' before doing anything else.

Analyze the situation and take appropriate action. This is a reminder not to jump to conclusions, not to rush to a 'fix' before considering all available information. It reminds us to prioritize among the various problems we're facing and be deliberate in how we solve them. In the absence of guidance, it's designed to remind us to think things through before acting, to give us the best chance of making high-quality decisions.

Land as soon as conditions permit. This instruction prompts us to figure out options for getting back on the ground, which may involve landing someplace we might not normally consider. This step of handling a situation encourages us to think about the range of possibilities, not just center on continuing business as usual. It also nudges us to do something—to bias for action—as opposed to endlessly deliberating possibilities. In these life altering situations, time is not on your side. You have to make a decision, and you only have so much fuel before indecision becomes your decision.

- Maintain aircraft control.

- Analyze the situation and take appropriate action.

- Land as soon as conditions permit.

In the hours following my cancer diagnosis, my wife and I began developing a plan to keep the family together and flying while we began the battle to regain my health. Together we determined a means of maintaining control of our family.

We analyzed the situation and took appropriate action. We decided who was going to perform my surgeries, which

"

There is no such thing as the perfect mission.

"

drove the location where they would be performed. We built a 'home team' support plan and organized to have both of our mothers come to Germany to help us with our kiddos. We developed our own crisis checklist and vowed to follow it.

And then we sought to land as soon as conditions permitted by finding a new place to land. We decided to retire early from the Air Force and come home to the United States, returning to our extended family and building stability in the event that cancer would return. As tempting as it was to keep going with a military career that was in high gear, we decided it was more prudent to 'land now' in an unplanned destination.

THE FUNDAMENTAL ETHIC

If there's one thing we learn and routinely experience in flying operations, and especially in flying single seat fighter aircraft, it's this: no mission ever goes as planned. And there is no such thing as the perfect mission. All we can do is deal with circumstances as they unfold and make the most of our circumstances.

Our ethic in the fighter squadron when the chips are down, when the plan falls apart and circumstances get away from us, is that 'the story just got better'. It's suddenly a much better story when we can talk about how we won, even when our team was down a couple of members and the enemy outnumbered. It's a much better story when we can talk about winning, even though our leader didn't make it to the day we execute our most important plan, even when we didn't have enough gas, missiles, tools, resources or whatever it is we would have normally needed to win as envisioned.

Our understanding is that we're still going to win—not doing so is not an option.

How we move out to win is what sets us apart. We have the approach that enables us to make high-quality decisions to help us solve the right problem the right way at the right time. We learn to keep calm in the midst of stress and to find a way to land, even when the circumstances are dire. And the notion that failure is not an option when facing certain challenges is what compels us to find a way even in the midst of disruption and uncertainty.

- When disruption hits, when things start to get hectic, remember:

- Maintain aircraft control.

- Analyze the situation and take appropriate action.

- Land as soon as conditions permit.

When the plan we orchestrated begins to fall apart in execution, we need to take a minute to breathe. We need to take the time we may not feel we have to make sense of the uncertainty we're facing. And once we've allowed ourselves to think, to make sense of our new reality, we need to deliberately develop our bias for action. We'll do so while recognizing not all of our decisions will be the best...but we'll recognize as well that we can still regroup and ultimately still find a good place to safely land.

We must embrace the idea that instead of being on the verge of collapsing our story, we can develop a way to make the next chapter even better. And as you get better, enjoy the fruits of successfully leading through our disruption and coming out stronger on the back side. Through these challenges, the story of my life, my family, and my future just got better!

POINTS TO PONDER

10.1   Have you ever felt a 'panic moment' of a trauma setting in? If so, what were your initial actions and thoughts?

10.2   How does your team initially (and collectively) respond to a crisis?

10.3   To 'land', you must understand what the minimum level of success is in each situation. Do you define success in every venture and effort?

CHAPTER 11

WE GROW BETWEEN THE (RESUME) LINES

Perspective & Insight of
Daniel Walker

I was not born this way; I grew into the person, the husband, the military officer, the leader, the Harvard Law student I am now. Years of work and training provided me the necessary repetitions to improve as I aged. Every so often, I have needed to apply to a job or a school that required the obligatory update to a simple 8.5x11 piece of paper highlighting my milestones along the way. These resumes or the more en vogue (certainly more Latin) curriculum vitae (CV) display the

"

*At no stage in my life was
I ever talented enough to
completely avoid failure.*

shiny pennies and brass rings of our personal history. They reveal to the reader all the cool places I've been, the machines I've flown, and the books I've probably read. Ultimately, these documents are mere snapshots that eliminate the element most critical to my growth, those that truly reveal who I have become: my failures.

And why would they? We all spend hours on our resumes trying to convince an HR department or admissions committee that the only mistake we've made is not applying sooner! That we've only learned through the sweet taste of victory, and excellence is our default state of being. Go us! However, the truth about my highlights is that each of them punctuates some failure or shortcoming that occurred somewhere between the lines. And in those gaps lie the real reason I am proud of my resume. My bullet points represent a willingness to continually learn and achieve through setbacks. All of them put together tell an even more important message. They acknowledge that at no stage in my life was I ever talented enough to completely avoid failure. At best, I have only ever been good enough to get somewhere; requiring that I needed to learn enough to stay, and eventually progress.

I was a good enough Air Force Academy cadet to be selected for pilot training, during which I needed to fail forward into being a real aviator, learning hard lessons but pushing onward to the next task all the same. I was a good enough pilot trainee to earn a slot as an F-22 Raptor pilot, after which I failed forward plenty on my way to becoming a Mission

Commander and instructor pilot. Now, I'm sitting on the lawn in front of Langdell Hall—the Harvard Law School library— failing terrifically towards my law degree. I am here ready to find out what I don't know and what I am not yet capable of.

All I am sure of is that today I am not good enough to meet the challenges my life will impose tomorrow. Neither are you. But the aim is to be resilient enough to get good enough as fast as possible. 'Good enough' can mean a lot though. Some days it can mean better skills. Others, it can mean toughness or grit. Most days, it means getting better at figuring out exactly what people or tasks need from you, and how to get that to them expeditiously. Whatever the definition, I assure you that you will lack a necessary 'it' when you need it. That is the tragedy and beauty of our fallible existence.

Prepare yourself for this inevitability. Prepare yourself by anticipating your shortfalls. Endeavor to fortify your weaknesses. But understand if your weaknesses are tested before you get them all battened down, then failure—or at least struggle—is imminent ... and that's okay.

Now for the 'how'. It's simple: introspection. Introspection the only path to success. You must have a consistent internal check-in in order to know exactly where your next challenge will come. Further, for you to flourish at introspection, you must have two things: peace and quiet. Turn off the radio, your phone, and Love Island (not judging, I love it too). Walk somewhere quiet, sit down, and think. Think about a failure or a close call with failure. As you think about that event, try to recall what you were attempting to do, whether you did it or not, and why that result occurred. Your 'why'—maybe you were too shy, or the plan wasn't equal to the task, etc.—might be rooted in a personal weakness.

Consider that weakness and begin reviewing how others strengthen similar weaknesses in themselves, then start experimenting with solutions. My weakness at the Air Force Academy was time management. To strengthen it, I surveyed my friends and tried their methods until I found a few that worked. I transferred that habit—crowdsourcing approaches to success—to pilot training, making me a better student and quicker learner. This technique allowed me to focus on other weaknesses more closely associated with flying. I love my friends for teaching me those lessons.

All in all, this cycle allowed me to grow into a man eager and willing to grow some more. That's it. And that's all I want to be able to do. To me, that's all any of us can do. Grow. But if done right, there will come a day when you must jot your professional life down into a neat bulleted background paper, and the highlights will write themselves, hopefully earning you the right to fail gloriously onward and upward once again.

POINTS TO PONDER

11.1   What does 'fail forward' mean to you? How do you embed this principle in your life?

11.2   How do you anticipate your shortfalls and fortify your weaknesses?

11.3   Are you truly eager and willing to grow?

CHAPTER 12

GETTING TO COMMITTMENT

Perspective & Insight of
Jason Harris

Trust can be an elusive concept, one that takes time to build and yet can be lost in an instant. In order to create and cultivate trust, we must be committed to the outcome. We must be committed to doing the work of creating connections, which means we must be committed to making ourselves vulnerable.

Creating trust is about creating connections. In order to create connections, we must first communicate. Here's what is interesting about communication: it isn't all about transmitting. In order to communicate for effect, we must learn to truly listen and hear what others are saying. Once we learn to communicate for effect, we can then begin to have true conversations. Conversation leads to connection. From connection, we can forge commitment. And commitment produces accountability and trust.

What happens if we are not communicating effectively? In the absence of meaningful communication, people will devise their own narrative to fill the gaps in communication, conversation, and basic information. Therefore, particularly as leaders, we have to be committed to communicate and connect with our teams. In fact, our first priority when setting out to create an organization built on trust is to open the lines of communication with our teammates. We must engage in the most basic of conversations, with the intent of getting to know our teammates. Getting to know one another is a steppingstone to trust. As we communicate with them, we begin creating meaningful connections.

How many times have we heard words like 'authentic' and 'vulnerability' being tossed around? It's easy to become cynical, doubting if there's really any place for these concepts in business. After all, how is vulnerability going to help anyone cultivate a high-performance team?

Authenticity and vulnerability are essential to building commitment and trust through communication. These words aren't merely platitudes; they are tools required for building trust. We simply cannot reap the benefits of trust, commitment, and high performance without working with the tools of authenticity and vulnerability. Here's why: some time ago I

"

Creating trust is about

creating connections.

attended a leadership retreat. The purpose of the retreat was to encourage us to connect with one another in an effort for us to work together effectively. The retreat was designed to place us in an environment that would facilitate communication with each other, the sharing of personal stories, and learning more about ourselves in the process. At the time I was not at all enthused about the prospect of participating in Mickey Mouse games and 'trust falls'. I resolved to attend, listen, and do the minimum required to check a box.

I figured I had been afforded more than my fair share of leadership retreats and team building contrivances. I was certain I didn't need another opportunity to demonstrate vulnerability en route to what I presumed might be contrived dialogue. I was comfortable with the minimal knowledge each of these people had about me—I actually believed the less they knew about me, the better.

Day One: From the get-go, we were asked to lay out our expectations and outline what we, the board members, desired to accomplish over this short weekend. Out of nowhere— violating my own personal pact to say as little as possible—I spoke up, surprising myself in the process. I suggested that everyone should be willing and committed to being vulnerable, open, and honest. As I reflect back on this, I think I was hoping that if I convinced them to be vulnerable, it would lessen the chance of me having to be the one to do so.

As I reflect further, I realize that being open, honest, and vulnerable is an immensely challenging idea in reality. Most people are not comfortable opening up to others, sharing details about themselves that could lead to judgment, maybe even putting ourselves in a position to be ostracized. In retrospect, I have to admit that this was my fear: I was afraid of being judged. I was afraid of not being accepted for who I am.

At some point I made a quality decision to open up and share. I don't think it was an entirely conscious choice, but I quickly found myself being open, being vulnerable—being my authentic self. Once I fully committed to authenticity, I also found myself fully committed to others in the group. My peers joined in, and before long I realized we were all mutually sharing a vulnerable space with each other.

One of the observations I picked up on immediately was that I was scared to be vulnerable. I was afraid to open up a part of myself to others that I was not previously accustomed to sharing. I feared losing respect. I questioned my fear.

Maybe I'm afraid to open up and share a deeper part of myself because I don't want to be misinterpreted. Maybe I'm fearful because I don't want someone to judge me. Perhaps I'm concerned that once I do open up, people may no longer look at me the same way. I'm just used to people looking at me a certain way. People see me as this happy go lucky, jovial guy. And I am comfortable with that. All the while though, I have the same challenges as everyone else in the room. And, like them, I also have my own unique issues to deal with.

As I reflect on the results of that retreat, it's clear that being vulnerable with those we are planning to work with is the most meaningful way to build relationships and trust. The reality is that I walked away with a greater feeling of acceptance from my team than I had previously felt. Instead of losing respect, I felt MORE respected, especially for sharing my perspectives, opinions, and my personality at a higher level. I went home from that weekend much, much closer to my teammates than I had ever been before. Choosing to communicate birthed a deep connection, and the foundation for trust was laid. We understood each other, and we understood how to commit and be accountable to each other.

High performance military teams learned and forged these lessons a long time ago. The camaraderie we enjoy is a direct result of us communicating and getting to know one another. We know each other at a core level because we are with each other all the time. In the proverbial foxholes of combat operations, these bonds deepen exponentially. We communicate, we connect, and as a result we create commitment. These bonds lead to connection, commitment, accountability and trust.

Vulnerability offers us the gift of appreciation, respect for one another and it breeds authenticity. It forges bonds that in many cases will never be broken. Our vulnerability naturally leads us to accountability and ultimate trust. The same bonds can be forged in any team setting…as long as we're committed to communicating authentically and openly with one another. If we are willing to commit to communicating and connecting we will be able to open the gift of our vulnerability, unwrap and uncover who we truly are, and it's there we will find the gift of connection and authenticity waiting to be revealed.

POINTS TO PONDER

12.1   What will you do today, as a leader, as a team member, to begin communicating with your team?

12.2   How will you consciously work toward creating connections with the people you work with?

12.3   How will you create an environment that cultivates commitment? How will your connections lead to commitment? Will you take the first step, communication, to cultivate an environment of trust?

CHAPTER 13

ELEVATING PERFORMANCE

Perspective & Insight of
Kim Campbell

The most effective leaders never stop learning. To elevate our performance, we must continually strive to improve. And if we want to elevate the performance of our team, then we must also expect the same from our teammates—keep learning and focus on continuous improvement. That is how we reach our potential, how we excel and enable our team to be at their best.

LEADER OF CHARACTER FRAMEWORK

The Air Force Academy's Leader of Character Framework—a framework we teach future Air and Space Force leaders—defines a Leader of Character as someone who lives honorably, lifts others to their best possible selves, and elevates performance toward a common and noble purpose. A leader of character elevates performance by going beyond the minimum standard of performance and truly works to excel and transform how things are done. The Leader of Character Framework says, "The most outstanding leaders are always growing, developing, and searching for new ways to expand their capacities (and their mission) beyond the minimum standard of expected performance."

LEARNING FROM EXPERIENCE

As a young Air Force fighter pilot, I got the opportunity to participate in a top gun bombing competition. We each got six dummy bombs to drop on the range, no explosives, just a smoke charge to spot where the bombs drop. Our judges evaluated us on our parameters, such as dive angle and airspeed, and how close our bomb was to the target. So even if we got a bullseye, a direct hit, we could be penalized for sloppy parameters.

On the bombing range, we fly our airplanes in a rectangular pattern that helps us line up with the target on each pass. As I rolled my airplane to the left, I checked my distance from the target, glanced at the altitude in my heads-up-display, and checked my speed. Solid. I approached my final turn, and rolled hard toward the target, pointing my A-10 at the ground, and lining up the neon green symbology in my heads up display right over the target. I quickly checked my parameters again . . . altitude, airspeed, dive angle. All good. As my pipper (the center point of our computed bombing solution) approached the dummy tank, I pressed down on the weapons release button, just as the pipper overlayed the base of the tank. It was exactly where I wanted it to be. Then I pulled hard away from the ground, feeling the G-forces press against my body as I banked the airplane away from a simulated bomb blast.

"Shack Two," the range controller said over the radio, signaling that my bomb had made a direct hit.

Overall, my time on the range went well and I knew I had a good chance of winning the competition. Later that day, just before the awards ceremony, our weapons officer, who is one of the most experienced pilots in the squadron, found me in the hallway.

"Hey KC (my fighter pilot call sign), I just want to let you know you missed winning the Top Gun competition by one degree."

"By one degree? What do you mean I missed by one degree?"

"Your safe escape maneuver was off by one degree."

A safe escape maneuver means that we max perform the aircraft to get away from the bomb blast. And if you don't do it right in training, you get a significant scoring penalty. And with real bombs? The mistake is potentially catastrophic.

I'm sure the look on my face said it all. I was in shock. My bomb scores were good. Does one degree in training really matter that much? My weapons officer decided at that moment to reinforce something incredibly important that I would take with me for the rest of my career: . . . precision matters . . . small errors matter . . . close enough isn't good enough. We must always strive to improve. If we want to be competitive, we can't accept close enough. I learned the hard way that one degree really does matter, that always fighting to improve matters.

That was a tough lesson for an overconfident young fighter pilot! And I definitely spent a lot of time critiquing myself about that one degree. I had made a mistake that would cost me the top gun competition which, let's be honest, was a blow to my ego. But that mistake also changed the way I operated as a pilot—it instilled in me a fighter pilot mindset and a fight for continuous improvement.

I'm thankful my weapons officer wanted me to be better, to develop the drive to perform better. He impressed in me an ambition to elevate my performance and to elevate the performance of my team.

LEADING BY ELEVATING PERFORMANCE

Elevating performance can be an individual endeavor and a team endeavor. As leaders, we must recognize that we should never stop learning; we should continually seek out ways to improve our own performance through reflection, coaching,

Leadership isn't about the leader, but it certainly starts with the leader being willing to learn and grow.

and training. There are many ways we can learn and improve, and we should set the example for our team by continuing to learn and grow.

Over time, I realized the same concepts applied to my personal life as well. How could I be a better mom and wife? I was always looking for ways to learn and grow from others who shared their experiences with me. I knew I didn't always get it right, and I wanted to find ways to improve in my personal life as well. Leadership isn't about the leader, but it certainly starts with the leader being willing to learn and grow.

So how do we help elevate the performance of our team? It starts with a foundation of integrity, of holding ourselves and others accountable for their actions, and providing honest and open feedback. It also requires a desire to lift others by helping our teammates improve. We want our team to focus on continuous improvement, to have a growth mindset where they can learn from mistakes and failures. With that desire as our foundation, we are positioned to elevate the performance of our team.

We can also help improve the performance of our team by ensuring we have a common purpose. In Simon Sinek's book, *Start With Why*, he says we should start by explaining the 'why' behind what we do. When we start with 'why', we can then connect the team to our common purpose, our reason for being, and our reason for action. If we are aligned toward a common purpose and goal, and we understand our individual roles in achieving that goal, then we can work together to elevate our performance.

Elevating performance requires discipline to hold ourselves and others accountable, to take time to learn from our mistakes. When we hold each other accountable for our performance, we enable our team to perform at their best. It also requires teamwork to share lessons learned and our personal experiences with each other. If we believe in our mission, our common purpose, and reason for action, then we can achieve the high level of performance expected.

It turns out, I learned a lot of lessons as a young fighter pilot, and many of those came from mistakes I made. I'm thankful I had a teammate who held me accountable, who took the time to help me improve, and who believed in elevating my performance for the good of the team. When we live honorably and lift others, we cultivate the opportunity to elevate the performance of our team.

POINTS TO PONDER

13.1 What actions can you take as an individual to elevate your performance?

13.2 What actions can you take to help your team elevate their performance?

13.3 What is your team's common purpose?

CHAPTER 14

LIES THE ODDS TELL

Perspective & Insight of
Daniel Walker

Day one of pilot training (Undergraduate Pilot Training or UPT as we called it in the Air Force) held many formative, memorable, and entertaining moments for me. I looked around at engineers, airline pilots, and former fighter navigators and realized for the first time I was not the only one 'born for this'. Pictures of the planes we've dreamt of flying for most of our lives teased us on the dreary walls of the flight room. On that day we also received our first of many questions from our instructor cadre: who wants to be a fighter pilot?

My classmates—29 stellar people—and I looked at each other, wondering who'd put their vulnerability on the line first. At that time, we all knew only about 5%, or 1-2 of the 30 incredible people in this room, might be fortunate enough to have the opportunity to fly a fighter aircraft; and the only thing that stood between each of us and that success was each other. We also knew that to get into one of those cockpits, we needed to be truly collaborative and humble in accepting that if it didn't happen, then it wasn't meant to happen. But in that moment, the instructor pilots or IPs asked us to physically put our dreams against the reality of the odds. And in that moment, nearly all of us raised our hands. So, there we had it; a best 2 out of 28 chance to fly fighters. Terrible odds by any stretch of the imagination.

However, a peculiar thing happened as time went on and we began flying. Though the instructors never again asked us to 'show our hand' as it were, through conversation I discovered that people slowly withdrew themselves out of the running to fly fighter aircraft. Some, after flying aerobatic missions, discovered they hated aerobatics. Others decided their passion was flying airplanes that would give them a greater opportunity to travel and see the world. And still others found pulling Gs (high gravity maneuvers) painful; I fell into this category. We each took stock of the cons, compared them to the pros, and decided whether they were worth the dream. I stuck with fighters, while others found better for themselves in different airframes. The numbers dwindled quickly from the original 28, down to six of us who still wanted to fly fighters after the initial phase of training. Those same six pilot trainees went on to the fighter training track, and all of us eventually flew fighter aircraft.

Having witnessed this process, I often think back to all the words of caution I got before UPT. People said, "...careful pursuing fighters, only 'x' number get them," advice that made me look at my peers and think I had 28 competitors instead of 28 friends. To be frank, we were all reacting to previous pressures, influences, and advice, instead of training exclusively to be the best pilots we could be.

All these variables played a role in sorting individuals where they ultimately needed or wanted to be, rather than acting as a screen of talent; by virtue of training with the greatest air force in the world, we were all skilled aviators. So, in reality, I was never competing against 28 other students. At MOST, I was competing against five other students; and in reality...none of us were competing at all. The odds, then, of flying fighters was never one of 28. It was always one of one; me competing against me.

All that anxiety. All the pressure. All the prestige weighed me down under the force of chance. This precluded me from enjoying my training as much as I could have. I wasn't flying to enjoy flying, or even to be a safe and effective pilot. I was flying to beat the odds. It was purely a competition.

Since this lesson dawned on me, I've preached non-stop to my mentees that they should disregard the odds; after all, they lie. Do not dare refuse to do a thing because of the odds. Do the thing you've desired and prepared to do. If you desire a thing, you will likely apply the necessary passion and effort to properly prepare. If you prepare properly, you have satisfied the only variable that matters.

The other variables may be beyond your control, but they ultimately work in your favor. A number of people you think you're competing against may show up without real devotion or passion and then shy away from the work. Some will find out they chose the wrong pursuit, and others may simply lack the drive to put in the full effort. You will then find yourself competing only against other passionate and prepared people—people you shouldn't compete with at all. Those are the individuals you should lean on who share a mutual enjoyment of a common desire. Bond in that commonality and find fun in the challenge you are all undertaking.

The collaborative nature of those relationships will yield a better version of yourself, one who will likely have a more enjoyable time, and will probably beat the odds.

POINTS TO PONDER

14.1   Is there value in competition?

14.2   How do you encourage collaboration in a competitive environment?

14.3   What do we gain by lifting others in the pursuit of excellence?

CHAPTER 15

CREDO THROUGH WHICH WE LEAD

Perspective & Insight of
Robert Teschner

Whenever I reflect on my Air Force career, I'm filled with gratitude for one significant fact: I was blessed to have been consistently led by outstanding leaders, privileged to be taught by, coached by, and cared for by leaders who collectively were more interested in my development than their careers. My leaders were fighter pilots who, by credo and virtue, were more interested in team success than individual glory. And don't mistake an emphasis on caring as a lack of competence; they were the best of the best, literally the best in the world. Together they revealed the job of a fighter pilot was to become a teacher, someone who was skilled in the art of teaching others how to succeed. Becoming a teacher had implications for how to lead— they understood that our ultimate task was to serve others. Together they taught us that servant leadership means living the following credo: Humble, Approachable, Credible, a credo that has applicability to all levels of leadership.

HUMBLE

According to Merriam-Webster, the definition of *humble* is "not proud: not thinking of yourself as better than other people." Given this definition, let's consider its application.

At the team level there are all kinds of challenges, chief of which is that the team consists of human beings. These groups of humans often work in close proximity to complete tasks and fulfill responsibilities that enable the successful completion of projects. The work can be intermittently hard. People will have good days and bad. The team wins, and it also loses. There are celebrations after successes, and blame after failures.

Failure has become the part of the equation that is most interesting because many leaders have come to appreciate that a team learns the most by navigating failure. It's through failure that innovation is born. It's through failure that learning

It's through failure that

innovation is born.

takes place. And it's also by successfully navigating failure we develop trust throughout the team.

None of this can take place if pride or ego gets in the way. None of the upsides come to fruition if we, as leaders, think ourselves better than our teammates. Quite the opposite holds true—we may well break the bonds of trust, not learn as much or at all, and miss out on the opportunity to innovate if we can't get over ourselves.

Learning to embrace humility is a necessary precondition to navigating failure. It's also a characteristic that draws teammates toward leaders. Its absence, likewise, pushes team members away.

Embracing humility means learning to respect our teammates as much as we respect ourselves. Seeing each of our teammates as our equal means recognizing that we owe it to them to bring our best every day. When we don't, we have to acknowledge that fact; when we make a mistake, we need to admit it. The most expedient way to do so is to recognize our fallibility and to understand that we owe it to ourselves and our teammates to admit to it.

As leaders, may we learn to be humble always.

APPROACHABLE

I've known talented, brilliant fighter pilot instructors who were so full of themselves that it was just painful to be around them. Despite their knowledge and expertise, I avoided these people as much as possible because I couldn't stand to be in their presence. Somehow, they always made everything about themselves, and they made it clear how much better they were than everyone else. These people may have been able to teach, but because of their demeanor, attitude, and core ethic, I didn't want to learn from them. None of us did. As such, they failed as teachers and as leaders because they weren't approachable.

Then there were those who made it their mission to lift up their teammates, specifically those who were not nearly as skilled, may not have had the same natural ability, and were often struggling just to keep up with such a high performing team. The people whose mission it was to make their teammates better drew us to them. I wanted to emulate them—we all did. And these were the pilots who found their way forward in the Air Force, selected to promote to the next rank, and eventually lead their own organizations. These people were always approachable, and they loved it when we came to them with our questions, our concerns, and our challenges.

The best teachers are approachable and make it a point to let you know they're here to help you. I've seen the best leaders approach leadership the same way. They understand their mission is to lift up, support, encourage, and guide by sharing what they know and passing on their wisdom and expertise. They want to connect with their teammates to be able to help and position them to succeed. They develop relationships with each person around them and revel in the fact that each trusts them enough to want to learn from them. Always. They make it a point to share. Always.

As leaders, may we learn to be approachable always.

CREDIBLE

In my experience instructing and coaching I've learned it's extremely hard to be humble. It's even harder to teach someone to embrace humility. The good news is that as hard as it is, humility can be learned, and progress can be made. Credibility is a different animal, one that might be even harder for some of us to embrace than humility.

According to dictionary.com, *credibility* means "the quality of being believable or worthy of trust." The question then is this: how do we become believable or worthy of trust?

The short answer is that we must live the core values in which we believe. We commit to be honest with ourselves and with others. We must know our jobs well enough to do them better than anyone else, bringing forward a willingness and ability to step in and do the job in place of one of our teammates when needed. We have to do what we expect others to do, and we have to hold ourselves to the same or higher standard than we demand of our teammates. In short, we have to live our professional and our personal lives with integrity.

This is hard.

But it is hardest if we are unable to embrace vulnerability. The leaders I found to be most credible in my flying career were also the most vulnerable—they were the first to admit to their mistakes and weaknesses. In doing so they publicly acknowledged they were as human as the rest of us. In so doing, they acknowledged what we all saw and knew, meaning that they told the truth and weren't afraid of the truth highlighting their flaws. They also taught us that we would all become better by discussing and learning from these flaws… making us a stronger team. The irony is that the most credible leaders I learned from were the ones who were always the most real.

At the same time, these leaders were also able to deliver. They performed. They learned from their mistakes, and they were really, really good. They talked the talk and then they delivered. The bad leaders talked the talk, admitted to their mistakes and were vulnerable…but couldn't fly well. These pilots were liked…but lacked the credibility we demanded in our profession. What we needed at the end of the day were leaders who could deliver. I was blessed to have learned from a whole host of leaders who did.

May we learn to become credible. May we learn to be vulnerable, to admit to our mistakes and weaknesses in a way that promotes team learning. Simultaneously, may we also truly learn to deliver, to produce results.

HUMBLE, APPROACHABLE, CREDIBLE

These words are designed to serve as a mantra. They exist in this form to guide the leader to a more perfect state of leadership. They offer leaders a roadmap to success…one that demands effort, is difficult, and will possibly require navigating hardship and pain. But one whose fruits are teamwork and engagement, buy-in and perform. In short, this mantra is one that answers the question, "What is a leader?"

May we learn to be humble, approachable, credible always.

POINTS TO PONDER

15.1   How do you, as a leader, ensure you are humble?

15.2   How do you, as a leader, ensure you are approach-able?

15.3   How do you, as a leader, ensure you are credible?

15.4   How are you teaching others to be humble, approachable, and credible?

CHAPTER 16

WINGMAN CULTURE

Perspective & Insight of
Chris Stricklin

E lite teams share many attitudes, motivations, and principles…common components that enable consistent performance. For the combat-proven leaders who participated in this military mentorship mastermind, one of the concepts we examined several times was the culture of the elite teams we had been fortunate to be a part of across our military experiences. Culture remains one of the most elusive topics to define across corporate and military organizations alike. Culture is difficult because there is with no set construct and only attributes and indications to be mimicked from successful cultures into the ones we're working on. While no single action or construct will ensure a strong culture, one common driving attribute across the military that frames our culture of success is the 'Wingman Concept'.

From the first day of basic training, the Wingman Concept is instilled in every young military professional. Air Force Handbook 36-2618 provides details of our force structure and directs each Airman to know and understand the Wingman Concept: "Airmen take care of fellow Airmen. A good wingman shares a bond with other Airmen." While the Airman's Creed obligates us each to be wingmen first, "I am an American Airman, Wingman, Leader, Warrior." The Creed goes on to explain, "As leaders and warriors, in time of war or peace, each Airman, to the best of their ability, is responsible for ensuring the safety and security of their fellow wingmen." This concept evolved from the early days of air combat when Air Force Ace Francis S. "Gabby" Gabreski advised us, "The wingman is absolutely indispensable. I look after the wingman. The wingman looks after me. It's another set of eyes protecting you. That's the defensive part. Offensively, it gives you a lot more firepower. We work together. We fight together. The wingman knows what his responsibilities are and knows what mine are. Wars are not won by individuals. They're won by teams."

Those who have served understand the truth that this is not a wingman *concept* as academia titles it, but rather a wingman *culture*. The role of a wingman is derived from the

Wars are not won by
individuals. They're won
by teams.

basic fighting element of fighter aircraft. As Jester taught us in Top Gun, "You never leave your wingman." This is true in the real world; a fighter pilot never goes anywhere alone. The purpose of a wingman in aerial combat is to accelerate the success of the team by increasing safety and capability while amplifying situational awareness. Even more simply, the role of a wingman is centered around three main duties: 1) always be prepared for any task; 2) see what the leader does not, do what the leader cannot; and 3) do what the leader needs done before asked. Simplified even further, wingmen have each other's 'six', the area directly behind each other's aircraft where pilots cannot see for themselves. The bottom-line for wingmen: 'My life is in your hands and yours is in mine.'

Along these lines, one of the most crucial principles to understand in the Wingman Culture—to expand it across a corporate team—is accountable interdependence. This concept involves developing a culture in which we hold both ourselves and each other responsible for performance expectations. Accountable interdependence is critical to executing well, with the goal being to be the best we can while delivering performance that continually outshines our nearest competitor.

A culture of accountable interdependence begins with each member truly understanding the joint dependence of each person's responsibility to deliver quality work with the highest standards of excellence. No one of us can succeed without all of us succeeding. Another way of understanding this concept is to say, "If one of us fails, we all do." (Katzenbach and Smith, *The Wisdom of Teams*) This concept was first detailed by Thomas Reid in his 1785 work, *The Intellectual Powers of Man*, when he explained:

A fiefdom of this kind resembles a chain, of which some links are abundantly strong, others very weak. The strength of the chain is determined by that of the weakest links; for if they give way, the whole falls to pieces, and the weight, supported by it, falls to the ground.

This idiom apprises us of the earliest concept of a wingman culture. This positive interdependence suggests that each person brings an essential skill to bear, one required for our progress. Without each unique contribution, we will not succeed in our mission. Simply put, we understand each member of our team is not only required in order to achieve success, but is an indispensable asset in our quest to do so. Our alignment on a common goal and the knowledge that we each serve a unique and critical role solidifies a concrete reason for being. This also challenges each of us to be better tomorrow than we were today, both individually and collectively.

Accountable interdependence involves three interwoven aspects of action. First, each person must hold themselves accountable for being the best they can be in the performance of their duties. This covers both the skill exercised and the manner in which each person performs their duties. Next, each person must hold themselves accountable for enabling others to exceed performance expectations. This means understanding others' jobs to such a degree one can forecast how and when one's teammates will need assistance. It also means assisting them in growing their skill sets appropriately. Finally, each person must hold others accountable for both the passion and performance expected. Through this expected, understood, and required accountability, the team's interdependence will be solidified.

This accountability-rich culture must reside on a foundation of strong relationships augmented by clear communication and active listening. To be successful, a team must reside in a workplace that is psychologically safe for each person. This, in-turn, allows each member of the team to be vulnerable while actively engaging with one another. Together, the team empowers and enables one another to achieve higher levels of performance. This collective dedication to continuous improvement will propel the team to even higher levels of performance than it could ever achieve alone.

As a wingman culture develops, it is critical to remember being and having a wingman is a privilege and never a right. Being a wingman is a continually evolving and growing responsibility. It's a partnership based in trust that grows with wisdom, knowledge, and true transparency in each and every action, inaction, and interaction. The greatest value of a wingman is they see everything from a slightly different vantage point than you do; a wingman sees what you do not.

As we all strive to build elite teams in our business world, we must ask ourselves, in a world of individual promotions and performance bonuses, how do we ensure the group is more important than any one individual? At the Air Force Academy, we did this by flipping our performance standards to one that is team output focused. We learned to be part of a team, learning that the strength of any team is based on the individuals who make up the team. We had to work together to support each other if we were going to succeed. As leaders we must embody positive growth, ensuring each person is secure enough in their role to enable others to be better than they are, while continually striving to improve. As confident leaders, we must be characterized by focused energy, effective action, and benevolent compassion. Our leadership is ultimately not measured by the performance of the organization this year, but rather ten years down the road once those we've led assume senior leadership roles themselves. Our success MUST BE measured by our followers' performance as they take over the reins. The true measure of a leader is not just calculated by the success of their organization, but by the measure of leaders they influence and develop to follow in their footsteps.

As you look at your personal growth, the two questions to ask yourself are these: 1) Who has your 'six'? and 2) Whose 'six' do you bear responsibility?

POINTS TO PONDER

16.1   Is our culture such that we strive to be an elite team? Why or why not?

16.2   How does the culture around us encourage or deter the three interwoven aspects of action of accountable interdependence?

16.3   How do we define success in our organization? How should we?

CHAPTER 17

THE QUEST TO IMPROVE

Perspective & Insight of
Chris Stricklin

According to Harvard Business Review, a team is a small number of people with complementary skills committed to a common purpose with a set of performance goals and approach for which they hold themselves mutually accountable. While that definition seems simple, developing a high-performance team is an extremely complex and arduous undertaking. It is our quest as leaders, to prepare tomorrow for higher levels of success than today. As this work draws to a close, it epitomizes the dedication to continuous improvement

It is our quest as leaders, to prepare tomorrow for higher levels of success than today.

of five individuals who truly understand that common commitment drives collective performance. We whole-heartedly believe in the power of a rising tide. If we surround ourselves with incredible individuals, ones who motivate and encourage us to achieve higher levels of performance, we will collectively see our average performance improve. Life is not a zero-sum game; there can be multiple winners, and together we can empower, encourage, and inspire one another to achieve higher levels of performance. Together we will embrace change and raise the bar on performance and, in the process, harness the power of the rising tide to raise the level of all the boats in our harbor.

This initiative began as a group of transitioning senior military officers supporting one another through mentorship and a psychologically safe space to improve individual leadership and collective performance. While sitting around the discussion table in our leadership cohort, we genuinely asked ourselves one day what we could do to better prepare the next generation, a simple question every generation and level of a leader should ask. The collective answer was to put some of these conversations on paper to give future leaders a foundational handbook. As Aristotle informed, "The one exclusive sign of thorough knowledge is the power of teaching." Along these lines, we knew our journey was to fully understand how we led in order to teach others to be better than us, which ironically would help us be more deliberate in our own leadership. John Maxwell directed us in *Leadershift*:

Only teach what you believe—passion.

Only teach what you experience—confidence.

Only teach what you live—authenticity.

As such, we spent time reflecting, discussing, understanding, and questioning our principles to teach what we believe to be true. While we are confident this work generates more questions than answers, it is meant to spark creativity, insight, questions, and a quest to improve today and be better tomorrow. This is our journey of leadership, shared to accelerate and inspire yours. And like the quest to develop a high-performance team, we will always strive for continuous improvement in ourselves, our teams, our processes, and our performance.

Achieving high performance requires a team to be focused and motivated with the right people in the right seats at the right time. More importantly, it requires each person to understand their value to the team and be extremely confident in their abilities. This will enable, empower, and permit space for calculated risks. Ultimately, we each desire to be part of a high performing organization again, like the military teams that developed us into the leaders we are, one which puts as much faith in us as we put in them, one which provides the psychological safety for each person to truly spread their wings and soar to new heights.

As leaders, our quest is to truly unleash and enable our team's power to empower and inspire a new tomorrow, one which delivers the intrinsic satisfaction of accomplishment and ultimately confirms we made a difference in our work, our efforts, and our lives—and those of the people we lead. We must embrace the weight of those lives which bear trust and faith in our leadership to guide their careers.

Please do not think of this as the end of our book, but the beginning of yours. Challenge yourself to strive for excellence and enable those around you to achieve their true potential. While our livelihood may be measured by what we earn, rest assured our lives will be measured by what we give. The true measure of a leader is not the success of their organization, but in the leaders they influence and develop to follow in their footsteps. A high-performance team is aligned in their 'why', dedicated to their 'how', and proud of their 'what'!

#LeadIntentionally
&
#LiveIntentionally

We are what we repeatedly do.
Excellence, then, is not an act, but a habit.

Excerpt from *The Story of Philosophy*

BIBLIOGRAPHY

Edmondson, Amy C. *Strategies for Learning from Failure.* Harvard Business Review Online, April 2001, https://hbr.org/2011/04/strategies-for-learning-from-failure.

Clark, Timothy C. *The 4 Stages of Psychological Safety.* Oakland, CA: Berrett-Koehler Publishers Inc, 2020.

ABOUT THE
AUTHORS

Chris "Elroy" Stricklin, Air Force Colonel (retired), is the award-winning, best-selling co-author of *Survivor's Obligation: Navigating an Intentional Life* where he details his ongoing journey in life to survive and thrive through the trauma of an aircraft ejection as an Air Force Thunderbird. He is a highly sought-after motivational keynote speaker and a combat-proven senior military leader, retiring after 23 years of service, which culminated with CEO-level leadership of a 7,000-person strong, $7B worldwide organization. His unique leadership style and skill have afforded him roles as a partner in a Forbes "25 Best Small Companies in America" leadership consulting firm with impact across multiple Fortune 500 businesses. He now serves as the founding president of a first-of-its kind talent development and management organization, with leadership presentations and publications before millions of business leaders. Chris and his wife, Terri, have been blessed with four amazing children.

www.ChrisStricklin.com

Robert "Cujo" Teschner, retired Air Force fighter pilot, is the national bestselling author of *Debrief to Win: How America's Top Guns Practice Accountable Leadership...and How You Can, Too!* He is a former F-15C "Eagle" instructor at the prestigious US Air Force Weapons School. He is also a former F-22 "Raptor" fighter squadron commander. Now he serves as the Founder and CEO of VMax Group, a St Louis-based international training company. In this capacity, Cujo is a highly sought-after motivational keynote speaker and corporate trainer. His expertise leading high-performance teams enables him to bring high-performance team training into businesses of all shapes and sizes, helping drive buy-in, engagement, and performance. Cujo and his wife, Diane, are blessed to be parents to five beautiful children.

www.VMaxGroupllc.com

Kim "KC" Campbell is a retired Air Force Colonel who served in the Air Force for over 24 years as a fighter pilot and senior military leader. She has flown 1,800 hours in the A-10 Warthog, including more than 100 combat missions protecting troops on the ground in both Iraq and Afghanistan. As a senior leader, Kim has led hundreds of Airmen both at home and abroad in deployed locations. Most recently, Kim served as the Director,

Center for Character and Leadership Development at the Air Force Academy. Kim is a sought-after keynote speaker, sharing her inspiring story with business and corporate audiences about a life-changing combat experience while weaving in ideas and lessons about leadership, vulnerability, and courage. Kim resides in Colorado with her husband and two sons.

www.Kim-KC-Campbell.com

Jason Harris, Air Force Reserve Squadron commander and Lieutenant Colonel, is a dynamic thought leader, motivational speaker, military leader, and commercial airline pilot. Jason is an in-demand trust and leadership expert, having done work for the United States Air Force Academy's Center for Character and Leadership Development as well as being a facilitator for American Airlines, training hundreds of pilots on implicit bias, equity, inclusion, and diversity. He has been featured as a History Channel, PBS, and NOVA documentary host and aviation expert with publications in Forbes, national print media outlets and multiple podcasts recognizing him as an authority on trust, leadership and high-performance teams. Jason and his wife, Kathleen, reside in Colorado with their daughter.

Daniel "FuZZ" Walker is a former combat-proven F-22 Raptor Mission Commander and is currently a Juris Doctor candidate at Harvard Law School. His academic, combat, and leadership experiences have enabled him to connect with and inspire diverse groups of people across the nation, to include a recent 60 Minutes feature story. Walker will be attending Harvard Law School as a Juris Doctor Candidate in the class of 2024. Daniel and his wife, Kelly, have two amazing children.

Made in United States
North Haven, CT
07 October 2022

25152966R00095